Praise for *Iran's Long Reach*

"This work provides an excellent analysis of post-revolutionary Iranian politics. The author exhibits impressive historical knowledge, paired with the ability to place Iranian current events into a larger context that includes the Muslim world, regional politics and conflicts, and tensions with the United States. A substantial, well-written book."

—**Bahman Baktiari**, Director of Research, School of Policy and International Affairs, University of Maine

"Few American foreign policy challenges are as great as those posed by Iran, and few Americans understand Iran as well as Suzanne Maloney. Iran's Long Reach *not only provides unparalleled insights into the way the Iranian regime works but offers provocative ideas about how to engage Iran—and why we should."*

—**Philip H. Gordon**, author of *Winning the Right War: The Path to Security for America and the World*

"This book provides solid analysis of Iran's politics and its implications for U.S. foreign policy. Its is a valuable and instructive contribution for policymakers and general readership alike."

—**Vali Nasr**, The Fletcher School of Law and Diplomacy, Tufts University

"Suzanne Maloney is a sure-footed guide through the thickets of Iranian domestic and international politics. Iran's Long Reach *is a forward-looking primer about a country that promises to remain as central to the foreign policy concerns of the next generation of American political leaders as it has been for their predecessors."*

—**Gary Sick**, Columbia University

"Suzanne Maloney has written an insightful and sober analysis of Iran as a 'pivotal state' that poses a major strategic challenge to its neighbors and to the security interests of the United States. She captures the external factors that have increased Iranian influence in recent years and the internal contradictions that could dramatically alter Iran's path. She has also suggested sensible ways to engage a country that will remain pivotal for the foreseeable future because of its location, resources, and revolutionary ideology. Iran's Long Reach *is a valuable addition to the current scholarship on Iran."*

—**Barbara Slavin**, author of *Bitter Friends, Bosom Enemies: Iran, the U.S., and the Twisted Path to Confrontation*

Iran's Long Reach

Iran's Long Reach

IRAN AS A PIVOTAL STATE IN THE MUSLIM WORLD

Suzanne Maloney

UNITED STATES INSTITUTE OF PEACE PRESS
WASHINGTON, D.C.

UNITED STATES INSTITUTE OF PEACE
1200 17th Street NW, Suite 200
Washington, DC 20036-3011
www.usip.org

First published 2008

Printed in the United States of America

The paper used in this publication meets the minimum requirements of American National Standards for Information Science—Permanence of Paper for Printed Library Materials, ANSI Z39.48-1984.

Library of Congress Cataloging-in-Publication Data

Maloney, Suzanne.
  Iran's long reach : Iran as a pivotal state in the Muslim world / Suzanne Maloney.
    p. cm. -- (Pivotal states in the Muslim world)
    Includes bibliographical references and index.
    ISBN 978-1-60127-033-7 (pbk. : alk. paper)
    1. Arab countries—Foreign relations—Iran. 2. Iran—Foreign relation—Arab countries. I. United States Institute of Peace. II. Title.
  DS63.2.I68M35 2008
  327.17′4927055—dc22

                    2008016494

Contents

Foreword

For at least two centuries, Iran has been of primary concern to Western powers. During the nineteenth century and for the first half of the twentieth century, Iran was a battleground for the imperial ambitions and rivalries of the Russian/Soviet and British Empires. Because of the Russo-British influence, other European powers' interest in Iran was historically sporadic and temporary, as with Napoleon's effort to use Iran in its desire to conquer Russia and Germany's interest in the 1930s.

Throughout the Cold War, Iran remained a prize to win in the East-West rivalry. Since the advent of the Islamic Revolution in 1979, Iran has turned into a major political, ideological, and security challenge to the West and its regional allies. The dispute between Iran and Western powers over its nuclear program is the latest manifestation of this challenge.

Throughout the last two centuries, the question of how best to deal with Iran or—as put by Lord Curzon, the one-time British minister in Iran and Viceroy of India—with "Persia and the Persian Question," has pre-occupied the chancelleries of major global powers. The British vacillated between a policy of making Iran a viable buffer against Russia's imperial ambitions in the Persian Gulf and a policy of keeping Iran "moribund." Russia faced a more-or-less similar dilemma in its approach toward Iran. Ultimately, both empires decided on a strategy of keeping Iran weak, partly out of frustration with Iran's determination to retain a modicum of independence despite its extremely weak position. The refusal of the Iranian Parliament to ratify the treaty of 1919 between Iran and Britain which, despite some advantages, would have made Iran a virtual protectorate of Britain, best illustrates Iran's attitude. The same sense of frustration with Iranian obduracy was apparent during the crisis over the nationalization of Iranian oil by the nationalist government of Dr. Muhammad Mosaddeq in 1951, ultimately leading to the Western-sponsored coup d'etat of 1953, which toppled his government. Western powers also became impatient with the Shah's pretensions to regional leadership and his hawkish position on oil prices in the 1970s despite his pro-Western position and philosophy. The same feelings are apparent today in regard to Iran's position on its nuclear program.

The reasons for great power interest in Iran are fairly obvious. Historically, the most important reason has been geography and Iran's position as a country astride the Persian Gulf and the Caspian Sea and in the vicinity of Russia, the Indian subcontinent, Central Asia, Turkey, and the Arab World. Since the 1940s, the energy dimension and Iran's position as an oil- and gas-rich country has added to its importance.

However, geography and geology do not fully explain Iran's importance. Iran's history and rich and dynamic culture, with its ability to absorb external influences and make its own unique synthesis, along with the long-lasting, though often unrecognized, sway of its cultural influence, even during its periods of political decline, have made it a "pivotal state" in the Greater Middle East in every sense, as Suzanne Maloney aptly calls it. Indeed, in the last hundred years Iran has been a pioneer in political and intellectual developments that have shaped the politics not only of the Middle East but also of the Third World in general. These developments have included the Constitutional Revolution of 1906, the nationalization of oil, Iran's role in presaging the ideology of nonalignment—with its theory of negative equilibrium, its role in the establishment of OPEC, the Islamic Revolution, and the emergence of a robust Islamic reformist discourse in Iran. The last-named holds promise of offering Muslims a way of reconciling their religious values with the need to come to terms with modernity.

Despite their long involvement in Iran, foreign powers, notably those of the West, have often read Iran and its changing dynamics wrongly. They have tended to veer from romanticizing Iran and various Iranian figures to demonizing them; from simplifying its dynamics to reading too many nonexistent complexities into its social and political fabric. And they have focused inordinately on the influence of personalities that have ruled Iran rather than on more fundamental forces affecting the country and more lasting influences that determine its external behavior beneath its changing political vocabulary. In this regard, the continued influence of Iran's historical experience, its security concerns, and its quest for independence are especially important.

During the last two decades, a particularly distorted view of Iran and its internal dynamics and external behavior has led the Western powers to pursue a policy of isolation and containment toward Iran that has ultimately been damaging to their own interests. Clearly, in dealing with Iran, like any other country, a mixture of different policy options is needed. But by not offering Iran sufficient incentives, the Western powers have created a situation within which Iran has had nothing much to lose from ignoring the concerns of the international community. A good example of this nonconstructive approach is the opposition to pipelines carrying Caspian oil through Iran. More damaging was encouragement of the Taliban as an instrument to prevent Iran's influence in Afghanistan and Central Asia.

How to deal with Iran is still puzzling Western powers as it did Lord Curzon. Therefore, the publication of *Iran's Long Reach* at this time is especially fortuitous. It makes a significant contribution to the understanding of Iran's current scene, set against the background of its long history. It provides insights into the workings of Iran's political system, its foreign policy, and its potential for either creating difficulties for the West or becoming a constructive element in regional and global contexts. This highly readable, well-researched, and well-written book also offers useful advice on the best way to deal with this pivotal country in order to check its disruptive potential while harnessing its constructive capabilities. Suzanne Maloney's insights are particularly valuable at this critical juncture in Iran–West relations when the consequences of wrong decisions could be highly damaging, and therefore it is vital that the Western world understands correctly what is happening in Iran and the reasons for its development.

Shireen T. Hunter (Ph.D.)
Visiting Professor, School of Foreign Service
Georgetown University

Source: Map produced by the CIA, 2001. Perry-Castañeda Library Map Collection, University of Texas Library, www.lib.utexas.edu/maps/iran.html.

Iran's Long Reach

1

Introduction

At midday on Fridays in south-central Tehran, when the day of rest hushes even the city's normally deafening traffic, it is possible to walk along the streets lining Iran's largest university and hear the booming anthem of the revolution that shook this country, and the world, more than a generation ago. The refrain of *"Marg bar Amrika"* (Death to America) echoes from the congregation of Tehran's Friday prayers with sufficient regularity to remind Iranians and visitors alike of both the catalyzing impact and the unexpected endurance of Iran's Islamic Revolution.

Nearly thirty years have passed since Iranians gathered by the tens of millions in the streets of the capital and other major cities and drove their monarchy from power. Iran's revolution reshaped the country, the region, and Iran's interaction with the rest of the world, especially the United States. The majority of those living in Iran today are too young to remember this period, and yet as their 2005 election of an Islamic firebrand demonstrates all too clearly, the Islamic Revolution remains the defining narrative for Iran's political, social, and economic development. By virtue of its size, history, resources, and strategic location, Iran under any circumstances would hold particular relevance for U.S. policy, as it did throughout the 1960s and 1970s. But the 1979 revolution and the political system that it wrought have placed Iran squarely at the heart of U.S. security challenges for the past twenty-nine years and will continue to do so for the foreseeable future.

That revolution, and the chaos and internecine civil war that followed, established the Islamic Republic, arguably the world's first and only modern Muslim theocracy. It also established Iran as the epicenter of a wave of religiously inspired activism and virulent anti-Americanism that would eventually radiate through the region and among Islamic countries across the globe. "It moved us from the age of the Red Menace to the epoch of Holy War."[1] Since that time, Iran's society and its political dynamics have undergone an evolution nearly as dramatic and unpredictable as the events of its revolution, but its leadership remains committed to two singular dimensions of the state's legitimacy—its religious inspiration and orientation and its antagonism, even defiance, toward Washington's role as the sole remaining superpower.

---

1. Christopher Hitchens, "Iran's Waiting Game," *Vanity Fair,* July 2005.

Iran is inherently exceptional in both the Middle East and within the wider community of Muslim nations—its dominant Persian ethnicity and culture is not shared by most of its neighbors, nor (with a few notable exceptions) is its population's adherence to Shia Islam. Moreover, the amalgamation of sacral and secular authority in the Islamic Republic rests upon an unprecedented—and still unique—doctrinal gimmick that itself has inspired a relatively paltry number of advocates outside Iran's own leadership. And yet, in spite of the many anomalies that distinguish Iran from the Middle East and the wider Muslim world, its influence—political, economic, intellectual, and spiritual—within the region and the *umma* (the broader Islamic world) remains undeniable. Indeed, since his election to Iran's presidency in 2005, the fiery Mahmoud Ahmadinejad has won legions of admirers across the region, using a combination of provocation and populism to transcend the ethnic and religious antipathies that traditionally have divided Iran from its neighbors.

Iran's influence is as multifaceted as it is profound. Its strategic outlook and ideological posture dictate the security environment in the Persian Gulf; through its support for terrorism and pursuit of weapons of mass destruction, Tehran remains the foremost challenge to the regional status quo as well as to vital U.S. security interests there. Economically, too, Iran remains a powerhouse despite three decades of U.S. sanctions and its own leadership's disastrous economic management, thanks to its endowment of 11 percent of the world's petroleum and the world's second largest deposits of natural gas, and its location at the crossroads of Asia's historic trading routes. As the center of gravity for the worldwide community of Shia Muslims and the heir to the ancient Persian empire, Iran exerts unique sway over a diverse and dynamic cultural sphere.

As a result of these multiple layers of identity and influence, Iran offers a compelling case for examining its role as one of the pivotal states in the Islamic world. First outlined in a 1996 *Foreign Affairs* article by Robert Chase, Emily Hill, and Paul Kennedy, the "pivotal states" thesis was offered as a means of organizing America's national security strategy in the post–Cold War era.[2] In lieu of a compelling Soviet threat, the authors suggested that Washington might best address the diffuse challenges facing U.S. interests by focusing its energies on particular developing states that, by virtue of size, history, and other factors, pose the potential to wield disproportionate influence over their respective regions and the international system.

Chase, Hill, and Kennedy delineated several criteria in their definition of a pivotal state. Most importantly, it should bear geostrategic value with respect to U.S. interests. Secondly, a pivotal state is one that is "poised between potential success and possible failure"; this uncertainty positions a

---

2.   Robert S. Chase, Emily B. Hill, and Paul Kennedy, "Pivotal States and U.S. Strategy," *Foreign Affairs* 75, no. 1 (January–February 1996): 33–51.

pivotal state as capable of helping and/or harming the region. Finally, the pivotal state should have carved out a significant role in global issues and negotiations. By investing U.S. attention and resources in such regional heavyweights, the authors argued, Washington could benefit from the multiplier effect of their leverage. Notably, the authors excluded Iran from their own short list of pivotal states, arguing that as a "rogue state," it already receives considerable U.S. attention.

Today, the impetus to articulate an intellectual imperative around which to focus U.S. security strategy seems quaintly obsolete. Five years after the "pivotal states" theory made its debut, the September 11 attacks clarified U.S. security priorities in tragic fashion and shattered any prior assumptions about the relevance of the developing world. Since that time, the exigencies of the global war on terrorism have trumped all other strategic principles, with considerable, though not universal, consensus.

Nonetheless, one can argue that the pivotal states framework remains a useful model for approaching the particular challenges facing the United States even in the aftermath of 9/11, particularly as it is applied in this series to that subset of the developing world that is linked in ways both amorphous and inextricable by a shared religious heritage. The terrorist attacks on American soil made painfully clear the shortcomings of America's existing strategic bargain. The illusion of stability had enabled Washington to disregard the means that its allies used to ensure it—the violent repression of opposition forces and the tacit export of militancy. And it shrouded a deeper danger, the failure of modernization in the Islamic world to generate greater public prosperity and a more liberal political order. Practicalities, politics, and principles resist any return to the old implicit strategic approach. In its place, a wide range of policymakers, pundits, and academics have argued for the promotion of meaningful political and economic reforms as the fundamental tenet for a new U.S. approach to the region. To implement that new approach, however, some mechanism for prioritizing the challenges and opportunities is essential. By focusing U.S. efforts on the pivotal states of the Muslim world—those countries whose futures are not yet certain but whose dynamics endow them with clout beyond their borders—we can hope to secure a better future for our vital interests in this domain.

Iran as a Pivotal State in the Muslim World

This monograph endeavors to outline the centrality of Iran and its ongoing political, economic, security, and theological dilemmas to the evolution of the broader Muslim world. This introductory chapter presents an overview of Iran's current political dynamics. From 1997 to 2005, Iran's politics were dominated by the promise of progressive change, although for at least half of that period it was evident to most Iranians that the promise had already been broken. Still, as long as the avowedly reformist president Mohammad Khatami remained in office, the political formula that his proponents had devised—the gradual usurpation of government institutions by reform-oriented politicians—appeared to be the single mechanism for altering the domestic and international course of the Islamic Republic. With the 2005 election of hard-line president Mahmoud Ahmadinejad, that blueprint for change has been made irrelevant, and a new era of contention between the orthodox defenders of Iran's Islamic Revolution and the forces of change has begun. The introduction examines this recent history as context for the later analysis.

Chapter 2 examines Iran's sources of influence on the broader Muslim world. Through its strategic ambitions and dynamism, political innovations, economic clout, religio-cultural institutions, and historical and cultural linkages, Iran is a driving force in the Islamic world—owing initially to its role as the progenitor of state-sponsored political Islam and more recently as the incubator of religiously oriented political reform. The Islamic Revolution bequeathed a multifaceted legacy that has made Iran a central player in the narrative of the region and the wider community of Muslim states.

Chapter 3 analyzes the social, economic, and regional forces that are driving Iran toward change. Although its leadership and rhetoric often appear stagnant, Iran is in reality one of the least static societies in the Muslim world. Thanks to a disproportionately young population and an economy subject to considerable external pressures and cyclical fluctuation—as well as the massive transformations occurring along its borders with Iraq and Afghanistan—Iran today is fraught with pressures and tensions. This section explores those frictions and examines the likely scenarios for change within Iran, and what a changing Iran might mean for the broader Islamic world.

Chapter 4 considers U.S. policy options toward Iran, recognizing the inherent limitations on our influence after a three-decade absence from Tehran but also the significance of Iran's role in the broader Muslim community of nations. If in the aftermath of 9/11 U.S. foreign policy was inextricably tied to the promotion of change in the Islamic world, then it is essential to understand how its critical actors, such as Iran, might be influenced in the foreseeable future. Ultimately, the United States is constrained by a variety of historical, legal, and practical factors. But if the project of democratization in the Middle East and liberalization in the broader Muslim world is to be successful, it will have to engage Iran and both sides of the energetic debate over religion, politics, and modernity in that country.

Iran Today

The Islamic Republic owes its longevity to an intricate balancing act between theocracy and democracy—between the power of the supreme (religious) leader, who holds ultimate and ostensibly divine authority, and the legitimizing force of the popular vote, which has featured prominently in the present Iranian system of rule. This dual and dueling structure of government reflects the contradictory demands of the broad revolutionary coalition that coalesced to topple the Shah. The constituents of this coalition shared little beyond their intense frustration with the monarchy; their interests, motivations, and visions for the postrevolutionary state diverged substantially and, in some cases, placed them in direct confrontation with one another. The result was a unique framework of competing institutions that facilitated the regime's religiously ordained repression at the same time as it nurtured the democratic aspirations of its citizenry.

The contention among the revolutionary coalition also conditioned another key attribute of the Islamic Republic—the entrenched competition among the Islamic Republic's political elite. From the start, the regime has been riven by infighting that persisted and even intensified after each successful purge. Even at the peak of its powers, Iran's Islamic government never achieved the totalitarian domination of its adversary Saddam Hussein. While Iran's dissension was frequently discounted as mere intra-elite squabbling, the regime's fierce battles and profound philosophical differences on such key issues as economic policy helped to preserve political space for debate.

From these structural and philosophical tensions emerged Iran's recent experiment in democratic reform. To the surprise of many Iranians and observers, the regime's splintered authority and vicious power struggle generated what in retrospect must be acknowledged as a serious and authentic effort to reconcile democratic institutions and values with Iran's self-imposed Islamic constraints. In one of Iran's many ironies, this reform movement had its roots in the regime's attempt to impose greater control over its fractious institutions, with the 1992 orchestrated ouster of many left-leaning officials by then-president Akbar Hashemi Rafsanjani. Hoping to facilitate the smooth acceptance of his economic restructuring and reconstruction package, Rafsanjani deployed the vetting authority of one of the key clerical oversight bodies to rid the Majlis (parliament) of rivals who did not share his own enthusiasm for private enterprise.

This faction, then referred to as the "Islamic left," found itself suddenly sidelined on the margins of the state that its members had helped create. From their refuge in universities, think tanks, and semigovernmental institutions, the Islamic leftists began to reassess their handiwork, recognizing in their own political isolation the absolutism and capriciousness that represent the systemic flaws of the postrevolutionary state. In their writings and debates, Iran's Islamic leftists questioned the increasingly domineering tactics of the regime, and identified the reassertion of the revolution's republican ideals as the solution to the country's enduring political problems. In order to advance their vision, the leftists also began plotting their way back into political power, reactivating old networks and developing strategies that reflected their emphasis on the state's elected institutions.

The left wing's reconsiderations coincided with the coming of age of a new generation of Iranians, whose expectations and sense of political entitlement had been framed by their rearing under the revolution. Changes in the social fabric of the country—in Iran's demography, its educational patterns, and its prevailing cultural constraints—made it inevitable that the latest round of the Islamic Republic's power struggle would transcend the limited parameters of elite politics. Youth participation combined with left-wing strategizing set the stage for the 1997 election of President Mohammad Khatami, a moderate cleric who had been forced out of Rafsanjani's cabinet into the relative obscurity of the National Library. With that election, the reform movement officially burst onto the national and international consciousness.

The Limited Legacy of the Reform Movement

Khatami's unexpected landslide heralded an explosion of political ferment and a modest relaxation in Iran's strict social and cultural taboos. His talk of civil society and rule of law triggered hopes that Iran's revolutionary juggernaut might finally yield to the aspirations of its citizenry. In diplomatic circles, the Khatami era augured the rehabilitation of the Islamic Republic and its commercial and political reengagement with the world. On the streets, Iranians invoked the date of Khatami's victory, the second day of the Persian month of Khordad, and the magnitude of his popular mandate, twenty million votes, as mantras for a better future.

It appeared briefly that this future might be within reach. In the first two years after Khatami's inauguration, changes in the permitting process facilitated the quadrupling of the country's press, helping to politicize a new generation of Iranians and challenge its prevailing orthodoxies and oligarchies. Social liberalization also accelerated, as evidenced by the increasing liberties taken in interpreting Islamic dress codes and by the raucous public celebrations that erupted in November 1997 when the national soccer team qualified for the World Cup.

Political changes proved to be a much tougher fight, but here too, the reformers made headway at the outset. Insistence on rule of law propelled the Khatami administration to investigate a series of dissident murders and, for the first time since the revolution, to force small but meaningful reforms on the Intelligence Ministry. By implementing long-disregarded constitutional provisions for local elections, Khatami expanded the country's democratic institutions and dispersed some authority to Iran's provinces. Internationally, reformers trumpeted the distinctly tolerant notion of "dialogue among civilizations"; initiated overtures to the United States, including the landmark 1998 CNN interview in which President Khatami called for "a crack in the wall of mistrust"; and intensified Iran's rapprochement with Europe and its neighbors.

The reformists also set about to rapidly and dramatically expand Iran's media, a deliberate strategy intended to generate broader public participation in the nation's political debates. The newspapers served as proxies for other forms of political activism that remained proscribed under the Islamic Republic's strictures. "The press was never intended to be the spearhead for Khatami's political reforms," former press deputy Bourghani acknowledged, "but it was soon apparent that it offered the fastest path to political liberalization."[3] One of the most prominent and determined reformist editors, Hamid Reza Jalaiepour, described frankly his decision to open a newspaper rather than establish a political party; having been denied a license for a political party, he acted strategically to exploit the opening granted to the press by Khatami and his liberal cultural minister. "Instead, I saw that press licenses were easier to get, so I opened a newspaper."[4]

The systemic transformation that the reform movement appeared to herald was to prove illusory, however. Throughout his two terms in office, Khatami and the reformists found their vision of a kinder, gentler Islamic Republic thwarted at nearly every turn by conservatives, who mounted an ardent defense of the system. Conservatives considered this reform movement anathema; the central tenets of its agenda affronted their vision of an Islamic moral order and threatened to undermine the theological foundations of the state. Through their control of the judiciary, the security forces, and key legislative bodies, the conservatives struck back with a vengeance to parry the reformers' public appeal. They shuttered reformist newspapers, obstructed Khatami's legislative program in the parliament, and filled Iran's prisons with a new generation of dissidents. Indeed, the reformists' greatest triumph—an overwhelming victory in the February 2000 parliamentary elections—immediately brought about a crackdown that progressively stripped the reform movement of its strategists, its initiatives, and its popular mandate.

The ensuing four years were dominated by political paralysis and a bitter struggle for power. Conservatives consistently eroded the authority of Iran's elected institutions, while the reformers' victories at the ballot box were made almost meaningless because all their savvy strategizing was unable to trump their rivals' monopolization of ultimate decision making. Meanwhile, reformers came under new pressure from students and liberal dissidents, who demanded more aggressive efforts to advance their cause.

---

3. Kaveh Ehsani, "'The Conservatives Have Misjudged': A Conversation with Ahmad Bourghani," *Middle East Report* 212 (Fall 1999): 37.

4. Afshin Molavi, "Extra! Extra! Extra! Iran's Newspapers at War," *Washington Post*, August 30, 1999.

After the brief honeymoon period of the late 1990s, neither the president nor his reformist cohorts ever proved capable of outwitting their adversaries or willing to risk a confrontation that might threaten the system. These disappointments cost the reform movement dearly in terms of its single historic asset, its popular mandate. From Khatami's May 2001 reelection to the second round of local council balloting less than two years later, voter turnout dropped dramatically, and those who did cast ballots heavily favored conservatives. This trend held true for the parliamentary election, which took place in February 2004, which was framed by another intense battle between reformers and the conservative oversight body, the Guardians' Council, which disqualified more than three thousand candidates from competing, including eighty members of parliament (MPs). The latter indignity finally provoked the reformers to engage in a rare and overdue protest, but their sit-in at Iran's historic parliament building failed to mobilize significant public sympathy.

The End of Managed Change

In June 2005, Iran experienced "a new Islamic revolution"[5] with the ascension of little-known hard-liner Mahmoud Ahmadinejad to the presidency. Ahmadinejad's unexpected victory undermined much of the conventional wisdom about contemporary Iranian politics, demonstrating yet again that the Islamic Republic retains considerable capacity for political surprises. Chief among those surprises was the evidence that Iran's conservative faction could, in fact, attract respectable levels of support from a population that profoundly resents its ruling system, and that it could do so not by moderating its revolutionary rhetoric but by projecting integrity to a cynical and disaffected citizenry. Although it is reasonable to suspect that Ahmadinejad's dark-horse victory might have benefited from some direct assistance at the ballot box or, at the very least, some undue influence, it is also clear that his candidacy tapped into a previously unexploited imperative among the Iranian people—the basic human desire for a better life.

Ahmadinejad's victory was significant not simply because of who won, but also because of who lost. In both the first-round balloting and the run-off election one week later, Iranians explicitly voted against the candidate who promised them democracy. Naturally, voters had sufficient justification for doubts that any candidate could or would deliver on such promises; still, the notion that the electorate in an autocratic system would spurn the candidates who criticized that system confounds some very basic assumptions that inform current U.S. policy. Of course, Iranian voters' rejection of democratic

---

5.   "Ahmadinejad Calls His Victory a 'New Islamic Revoltion,'" *Associated Press,* June 30, 2005.

enticements was made in favor of an alternative, and evidently more compelling, offer—that of material improvements to their daily lives.

In the first round of the elections, this national compromise generated a surprisingly high turnout for Mehdi Karrubi, one of the stalwarts of the early revolutionary years who served several stints as parliamentary speaker. His presidential pitch centered around a pledge to distribute Iran's oil bounty in the form of a monthly stipend to each Iranian adult. This $60-a-month promise netted Karrubi an unexpected third place in the official tally, and a credible complaint that an accurate count might have placed him higher. Finishing a distant fifth was Mostafa Moin, the earnest but unexciting former Khatami cabinet minister who had run as the official candidate of the reformist movement. Iranians were sympathetic but ultimately unconvinced by Moin's increasingly frantic effort during the campaign to outline an agenda that was ambitious but promised little prospect for implementation.

With only a week to refocus energies on the competition between the top two vote-getters, the second round of voting proved even more dramatic. It was a study in contrasts—Akbar Hashemi Rafsanjani, Iran's savviest power broker, taking on the rumpled, unknown Ahmadinejad. To win back the position he had held for two terms in the 1990s, Rafsanjani launched a slick, cynical campaign that was buttressed by the last-minute backing of reformist politicos desperate to avoid what they advertised to the Iranian people as the onset of fascism. But voters scoffed at Rafsanjani's claims to have supported reforms, and opted overwhelmingly in favor of yet another electoral upset.

Ultimately, Ahmadinejad benefited from the well-organized political machine that is the Islamic regime's base, and many Iranians reasonably presume that he was assisted by considerable electoral manipulations as well. Indeed, with varying degrees of directness, at least three of the erstwhile contenders for the presidency alleged serious improprieties and demanded a government investigation. However, beyond whatever legal and extralegal electoral manipulations were deployed to boost him to power, Ahmadinejad managed to do what no preelection analysis suggested was possible—persuade a sizeable portion of Iran's electorate to endorse a candidate defending the status quo political system. What resonated most about Ahmadinejad's candidacy was his simple message, his upright reputation, and his focus on the hardships and inequities that afflict the average Iranian. In one of his final campaign appearances, Ahmadinejad spoke bitterly about the indignities of Iran's grinding poverty; upon his victory, he proclaimed himself honored to be "the nation's little servant and street sweeper."[6] Like the watershed 1997 election of Khatami, Ahmadinejad's victory represented a protest vote,

---

6.   Colin Freeman, "I Am Proud of Being the Nation's Little Servant and Street Sweeper," *Telegraph* (London), June 26, 2005.

a mutiny by an electorate more concerned with jobs and the cost of living than with lofty promises of democracy.

His victory also highlighted the paucity of alternative options available to Iranians. A push for a public boycott by Iran's inchoate opposition fell short of its goal of denying the regime the legitimacy of public participation. Here again, Iranians—particularly those outside of Tehran—demonstrated their unwillingness to break wholly with the system. The election, while not at all free and fair, at least offered an opportunity to make some sort of a choice. Iranians saw no strategic path for achieving a more attractive future that was sufficient to cede their limited role in charting their nation's course by boycotting in large numbers.

The balloting firmly closed the door on an era and a particular political strategy—one that posited a rehabilitation of the Islamic Republic through the restoration of the limited but potentially operational guarantees of representative government upon which it was established. The paradigm of change espoused by the reform movement—change from within the system itself—was not only discredited, but was deprived of any institutional vehicle to advance its aims. Today, across the board, the individuals who control all branches of government in Iran are committed to the preservation of the status quo.

Reform in Retrospect: Why a Mass Political Movement Did Not Succeed

Accepting the proposition that the reform movement's strategy no longer remains viable, it is fair to consider briefly what brought about its frustration. First, it is clear that the strategy itself was inherently limited by the moderate nature of its ambitions and the restraints that its leadership imposed on its quest to implement its agenda. Their cautious approach represented the authentic impulses of politicians who had spent two decades as part and parcel of the Islamic system and who were convinced that the changes they advocated represented an inevitable consequence of Iran's changing society.

Khatami and his allies were not naïve; rather, having battled back from political oblivion, many were profoundly cynical about the political system they were challenging and the prevailing political culture, which had condoned successive suppressions of popular rule. Iran's reform movement therefore explicitly set out to avoid any overt challenge to the boundaries of permissible political discourse ("redlines" in the Iranian vernacular) and to capitalize on the room for maneuver accorded the mainstream political elite. However, reform within the redlines failed to anticipate the intense reaction from the conservatives, who viewed these tactics as unambiguously threatening and responded in kind. The reformers' prudence may have temporarily preserved their place in Iranian politics, but it did not protect them or their agenda from vicious attacks. The conservative campaign ultimately made a mockery of the reformers' strategic self-restraint.

The second significant factor that contributed to the breakdown of the reformist strategy was the deeply held fear of instability and disorder that permeates Iran's political culture, a trait that may be the single most significant legacy of the Islamic Revolution. Khatami, for one, never demonstrated the stomach for high-risk gamesmanship, particularly after the shattering violence of July 1999, when security forces and hard-line thugs crushed student protests. Many influential reformers were convinced that their movement stood to lose more than it gained by casually wielding its most potent asset, its popular support. Rather than rally their supporters in the streets, MPs penned appeals to the supreme leader that were as eloquent in their appeal for democratic institutions as they were ineffective in achieving them. For his part, Khatami focused his energies within the bureaucracy—trying to advance legislation that would enhance the presidency's powers and check the authority of unelected institutions. "Mr. Khatami should have invited the people to, for example, Azadi Square to talk to them," Dr. Ibrahim Yazdi noted ruefully in 2003. "If he had invited them one year after his victory, nearly one million people would have gathered and it was enough to spark horror among the rulers. Khatami could not do so and it is a big fault."[7] As a result, successive electoral mandates were squandered and Iranians became disenchanted with the glacial pace of change.

Finally, the reform movement never fully transcended its elite origins, as evidenced in the movement's organization as well as its ideology. The reformers remained a cliquish group of political insiders (*khodi*, in the Iranian vernacular) who never managed to mobilize society in support of their efforts. As a result, even the Islamic Iran Participation Front—the largest and most geographically dispersed reformist group—registered only ten thousand members from Iran's seventy million citizens. Elite bias was mirrored in the movement's rhetoric and policy objectives, which presumed freedom to be the most sought-after social good, despite evidence that Iranians craved economic security at least as much as they yearned for liberty. The reformers' failure to make a persuasive case to address Iran's economic dilemmas contributed to the perception that its leaders were out of touch, and sapped the movement of some of its populist appeal.

---

7.   Mohammad-Mehdi Sofali, "The Threat Is Serious, Believe It!" *Nassim-e Saba* 99 (July 20, 2003): 6.

The Era of Ahmadinejad

If the 2005 presidential election marked the conclusion of the incremental-ist, insider strategy of the reform movement, it also represented the open-ing salvo of a new era in Iranian politics. The current phase is marked by the reascendance of the conservatives, who are clearly in command of Iran's near-term course, and the surprising centrality of Ahmadinejad him-self. After his unexpected electoral victory, the conventional wisdom pre-sumed the previously unknown blacksmith's son to be a political naïf and a mere pawn of his hard-line backers. The office that he holds is a deliber-ately weak one, thanks to the enduring suspicion of Iran's revolutionaries toward central authority and elective office, and Ahmadinejad's predeces-sors routinely found their agendas constrained by the post's constitutional and bureaucratic limitations. Moreover, Ahmadinejad had no real prior exposure on the national or international stage. As a result, most pundits initially predicted that he would have only modest impact on decision making, and have continued to anticipate that the president's days are numbered or his influence waning.

As happens all too frequently with Iran, the experts have been proved resoundingly and repeatedly wrong. Much as he may be resented by other Iranian politicians and reviled by most of his counterparts around the world, Ahmadinejad matters. He placed himself at the center of Iran's most conten-tious debates and at the forefront of its long-running antagonism with Wash-ington. At home, through an ambitious program of administrative over-hauls and personnel changes, he reshaped Iran's bureaucracy and altered a number of key policies. In the foreign policy arena, Ahmadinejad deftly exploited international opposition to Iran's nuclear program as a domestic rallying point, and his odious statements on the Holocaust and Israel have made him something of a regional icon, willing to confront Western powers and orthodoxies.

At least in part, his relevance can be credited to fortuitous timing. Ah-madinejad benefited from the rising tide of anti-Americanism and regional anguish over violence in Iraq and Palestine. He was also boosted by the July 2006 conflict in Lebanon, which enabled Ahmadinejad to mug for the masses across the Arab world even as it heightened regional leaders' concerns about Iranian troublemaking. Ahmadinejad has trumpeted the electoral victories of Islamist groups in Palestine, Egypt, Lebanon, and elsewhere in the region as evidence that his brand of politics is ascendant.

Equally important to his endurance, however, are Ahmadinejad's formi-dable political skills, which have too often been underestimated by his de-tractors at home and abroad. His limited experience in national and inter-national politics notwithstanding, the Iranian president has demonstrated a real talent for populist theatrics and bureaucratic gamesmanship, both of which have helped him outmaneuver his rivals. Chief among his political assets is audacity; his brash talk is mirrored by an unwillingness to be side-lined from key policy debates. Ahmadinejad's determination to play a central and public role in foreign policy has forced the departure of several key rivals, including Ali Larijani, who until October 2007 served as Iran's chief nuclear negotiator. This ambition and obstinacy has translated into greater practical influence than either his office or his stature would normally imply. Compared to his mild-mannered predecessor, Ahmadinejad has greater—albeit more negative—impact on the dynamics of Iran's politics, economy, and foreign policy by virtue of his unyielding ways.

Iran's controversial president has also profited from the quiet but apparently consistent support he has received from Iran's ultimate decision maker, supreme leader Ayatollah Ali Khamenei. Neither Ahmadinejad's domination of the public debate on key issues nor his persistence in the face of challenges from a variety of establishment elites would be possible without the approval, or at least acquiescence, of Khamenei. Their tacit alliance reflects both ideological and practical political considerations. First, there appears to be a convergence in their views on the centrality of Islamic values, which Khamenei has described as a sort of personal vindication after the reformist period.

> Perhaps some individuals, even some sincere members of the revolution and not the outsiders and ill-wishers, had come to the conclusion over the past several years that the era of the revolution's original slogans was over. . . . We knew that they were making a mistake. But their presumptuousness was painful to [our] hearts. Thanks to the Iranian nation's endeavor and the nation's choice today, a government has been elected whose principled and fundamental slogans are the same as the original slogans of the revolution. That is, the basic watchwords of the Islamic Revolution are the dominant and popular ideas today. This is highly significant.[8]

Like Ahmadinejad, Khamenei is inherently distrustful of the West and is convinced of the permanence of U.S. antipathy, a legacy of the formative influence of the Iran-Iraq war, which Khamenei has described as "not a war between two countries, two armies; it was a war between an unwritten, global coalition against one nation."[9] Like Ahmadinejad, Khamenei is prone to seeing a conspiracy around every corner, and he shares the president's

---

8.   Ayatollah Ali Khamenei, speech in Tehran on June 30, 2007, broadcast on Vision of the Islamic Republic of Iran Network 1 on July 1, 2007, World News Connection.

9.   "Supreme Leader Khamene'i Emphasizes Spiritual Strength of Iranian Army," Tehran Voice of the Islamic Republic of Iran Radio 1, April 16, 2003, World News Connection.

preference for offense as the best defense. "We need courageous actions," the supreme leader commented in July 2007. "And this is why I thank God for this government, that is, there is the courage for taking action."[10] Moreover, Khamenei is presumably more comfortable with a chief executive whose public appeal bolsters rather than threatens the legitimacy of the revolutionary system and his own office. In practice, Khamenei has repeatedly commended Ahmadinejad's administration in public for revitalizing the spirit and mores of the revolution, while chastening its critics in a fashion rarely seen during the eight-year onslaught by conservatives against Khatami.

Thanks to his implicit backing from Khamenei, Ahmadinejad at least for the moment appears to have outflanked efforts by his rivals to contain him. He has purged detractors from his cabinet, forced the resignation of powerful rivals such as Larijani and rebounded apparently unscathed from setbacks such as his slate's loss in December 2006 elections. While his influence on specific decisions is impossible to ascertain from the outside, Ahmadinejad has indulged in relentless self-promotion both at home and abroad. His presidency is quite a contrast from his campaign for the office, when he cleverly showcased his modest lifestyle, particularly contrasting his apartment in a low-rent district of Tehran with the grand villas of Iran's power brokers in the capital's posh northern neighborhoods.

Initially upon assuming the presidency, Ahmadinejad continued to project an unpretentious persona, rejecting the tradition of hanging the president's portrait in all state offices and dispensing with the new presidential jet. However, the president's personal frugality belied his ambition and his predilection for instigating drama in which he would play a central role. At home, perhaps the best example of Ahmadinejad's imperious presidency has been his well-publicized program of visiting each of Iran's thirty provinces, with his entire cabinet in tow and an open pocketbook for both personal petitions and public works. The president's nationwide tour, which has now entered its second round, has elicited more than nine million letters penned directly to the president, who claims to have adjudicated thousands of cases and provided 2.4 million Iranians with at least a token financial response. The visits have had two primary political payoffs for Ahmadinejad. First, they have bolstered his support from the supreme leader, who has praised the effort as a "very good and necessary initiative" while castigating the public criticism of Ahmadinejad's travels.[11] Second, the visits have bolstered the president's support outside of Iran's major urban centers, a segment of the country that has become increasingly relevant to securing elective office in Iran.

Ahmadinejad's presidency has also been marked by the increasingly prominent role of military institutions and individuals in Iranian politics. In

---

10. Ayatollah Ali Khamenei, speech in Tehran on June 30, 2007.

11. Ibid.

particular, the Revolutionary Guards have assumed a more prominent role in Iran's economy, securing key stakes in major projects including the energy sector, which until recent years remained the province of the state oil company and its affiliates. Additionally, a number of current and former Revolutionary Guard commanders have moved into the parliament and political posts across the Ahmadinejad administration, most notably in the Interior Ministry, which not only commands Iran's internal security forces but also is charged with implementation of elections. The expanded role of the military leadership in Iran's politics and economy represents a significant shift with respect to Iran's recent history of distinctly separate civil and military spheres of authority, although it is to some extent the predictable result of the eight-year war with Iraq, a formative experience for the postrevolutionary state and leadership.

The role of military commanders and organizations is complemented by what one expert on Iran's internal politics has described as the "security outlook" of the current leadership; in other words, "a newly security-conscious state, bordering on paranoid, has indeed emerged."[12] This heightened sense of suspicion and defensiveness appears to reflect both the innate predilections of the new configuration of power in Iran and the perception of intensifying American pressure. In a sense, the two factors have served to reinforce one another, particularly as Washington has singled out the Revolutionary Guards for targeted sanctions and financial restrictions.

Predictably, however, the resurgence of Iran's conservatives over the past five years has contributed to their fragmentation; having propelled the reformists to the sidelines, Iran's hard-liners are now fighting among themselves in a much more public fashion than ever before. Divisions within Iran's orthodoxy have existed since the earliest days of the revolution, but today they are exacerbated by the postrevolutionary generation's coming-of-age. Many traditionalists have been unnerved by Ahmadinejad's scathingly candid attacks against Iran's political insiders, such as Rafsanjani, as well as the presumably unintended consequences of his radical discourse and policies. "Someone who drives at such a speed should be more careful about his performance," observed Mohammad Reza Bahonar, deputy speaker of the parliament, on Ahmadinejad's call for officials to keep up with his fast pace. "If he does not foresee the obstacles in the way, the accidents will be even more terrible."[13]

And while Ahmadinejad is part of this new cohort of leaders, these younger conservatives are more diverse than is often depicted, and several

---

12. Farideh Farhi, "Iran's 'Security Outlook,'" *Middle East Report Online,* July 9, 2007, www.merip.org/mero/mero070907.html (accessed April 15, 2008).

13. Aresu Eqbali, "Iran Conservatives Slam Ahmadinejad on Economy," Agence France-Presse, December 23, 2007.

of the political vehicles associated with the younger generation hard-liners began distancing themselves from the president even before he took office. MP Emad Afruq, a conservative politician who originally chaired the current parliament's cultural committee, has become one of the most outspoken critics of Ahmadinejad, accusing the president's political faction of having "embraced a creed of religion-state union that does not make politics religious and moral. This creed makes religion and morals political and struggles for power in the name of religion and morals," adding that this tendency is more dangerous than secularism because it "taints the good name of morals and religion."[14] Such conservative splintering has helped dilute their influence at the ballot box since their 2005 apex, and the December 2006 elections for the Assembly of Experts and local councils were widely viewed as a rebuke to Ahmadinejad and a signal that the conservative reconquest of Iran's elective institutions would be neither permanent nor unchallenged.

For their part, Iran's reformists are beginning to reassert themselves on the national political stage, focusing their message on Ahmadinejad's excesses and seeking to reclaim some place within the country's elective institutions. The internecine debates within the reformist camp have largely been overshadowed by their shared antipathy to Ahmadinejad and his policies. By nominating a number of moderate members of the Islamic Republic establishment for the 2008 parliamentary elections, the reformists hoped to claw their way back to political relevance, assume greater influence in shaping Iranian policies, and position themselves to credibly contest the 2009 presidential election. As the results of that contest demonstrate, the conservative domination of the electoral system as well as the reformists' own strategic disorientation, a comeback for the Khatami camp is at best an iffy proposition. And even if they were to somehow regain a foothold in the Majlis or other state institutions, it remains unclear if the reformists can advance a common, positive agenda for Iran's future beyond their critique of the government.

Former president Khatami has emerged as an elder statesman for the reform movement, playing a central role in election strategizing and once again winning ovations from student audiences—a sharp contrast from the jeers he received at the close of his two terms.[15] Khatami's approach has certainly not been vindicated, but popular opinions of his presidency have risen if only by comparison with the current environment. Additionally, after vilifying him during their heyday, Iran's mainstream reformists also appear to have made their peace with Rafsanjani, and it is possible to envision Iran's

---

14. Emad Afruq, "Repulsive Stench from Electoral Competitions," *Etemaad-e Melli*, June 19, 2007, as translated by World News Connection, document number 200706191477.1_ 6fd800507af307ca.

15. See the analysis of Hamed Tabibi, "University Welcomes Khatami," *Etemad*, December 12, 2007, www.etemaad.com/Released/86-09-21/150.htm (accessed May 9, 2008).

politics moving toward a grand coalition of centrists, incorporating political actors from both ends of the political spectrum.

The most trenchant critiques levied by reformists as well as conservatives have focused on Ahmadinejad's handling of Iran's economy, an issue that will be explored in greater depth below. Notwithstanding the president's shrewd deployment of popular economic grievances to boost his standing at home, his administration has only exacerbated the underlying distortions that plague Iran's economy and has done little to capitalize effectively on the record oil windfall of the past few years. As a result, the conservatives in power now risk repeating their predecessors' blunders by raising public expectations of rewards that they have little prospect of delivering. Should Iran's government fail to live up to the minimalist expectations of a disillusioned citizenry, the relative quiescence of the Iranian population could well erupt into a much more serious challenge to the system and its legitimacy than the Islamic Republic has yet faced.

Many analysts have commented that the conservative reconquest of Iran's elected institutions will not usher in the end of reform in Iran simply because the movement emanated from social conditions that remain even more applicable today than in 1997. Iran's disproportionately young population, more urbanized and better educated than at any point in history, are just now coming into their own, and their impact will ultimately preclude any lasting return to the authoritarian impulses that dominated the Iranian revolution's first decade.

However, even if Iran's Islamic order is beginning to crumble thirty years after its inception, the state that it forged has proved ever more enduring. Although the rhetorical jousting over Ahmadinejad and the occasional evidence of popular backlash against the regime raises hopes that meaningful change is on the horizon in Iran, the reality is probably less promising. Throughout the Islamic Republic's history, its political elite have consistently engaged in fratricidal partisanship. One revolutionary stalwart commented recently that "what you see in relation to the supporters of Ahmadinejad, you need to look at the archives, as you would be able to find the same for the supporters of Mr. Khatami and Mr. Hashemi Rafsanjani in there."[16] This contested internal political battlefield rarely threatens the system's stability; rather, Iran's multiple spheres of influence and jockeying political factions ensure considerable consensus that is the hidden strength of the system.

Moreover, while there is broad-based antagonism toward the regime, there is no real opposition movement or a credible strategy for mass mobilization. For now, Iranians—though unequivocally frustrated and disenchanted with

16. "Asgarowladi's Criticisms of the Conduct of the Government's Supporters," *Etemad*, August 28, 2007, www. etemaad.com/Released/86-06-06/150.htm (accessed May 9, 2008).

the ephemeral promises of reform—have demonstrated that they are not yet prepared to take that frustration to the streets. Nor has an organization or potential leader yet emerged from the chorus of complaints that appears to have the discipline or the stamina to sustain a major confrontation with the forces of the government. Having endured the disappointment of their last democratic experiment going awry, Iranians are weary of political turmoil and, at least for the time being, resigned to a waiting game with respect to regime change.

Despite his manifest difficulties with both Iran's political elites as well as its population, it would be a mistake to presume that the era of Ahmadinejad is therefore on the wane. As Iran approaches a presidential election in mid-2009, the president benefits from the authority to stack the deck in his own favor, as well as from his patrons in the hard-line clergy, the Revolutionary Guards, and the supreme leader's office. Moreover, even if Ahmadinejad somehow passes from the scene, there is every reason to believe that the legacy of his ideological fervor and the constituency whose worldview he has represented—"neoconservatives" or second- and third-generation ideologues—will continue to shape the options available to any future Iranian leader.

Nonetheless, it is worth remembering that few analysts have successfully predicted the outcomes of Iran's routinely surprising presidential contests, including the upset victories of Khatami in 1997 and Ahmadinejad in 2005. This is partly a function of the profound limitations on our information and understanding of internal Iranian developments, but also reflective of the power of unintended consequences in shaping Iran. Its popular, peaceful revolution begat a vicious theocracy, and a decade later, the regime's attempt to marginalize opponents of its postwar economic reforms spawned a political and cultural reform movement. At a time when Iran is dominated by an unreasonable leadership and gridlocked internal politics, it is worth remembering that Iran's politics are likely to resist simple prognostication and to defy the expected outcomes.

Iran's Domestic Dynamics and Its International Approach

In its early years, the Islamic Republic's worldview was characterized by an uncompromising vision of Iran's interests as encompassing the umma, as well as by a revolutionary preoccupation with independence or detachment from great power politics. These influences molded an antagonistic Iranian approach toward the established states along its border as well as toward its former patron in Washington. From the outset, however, the nationalist underpinnings of Iranian foreign policy have continuously asserted themselves and assumed increasing primacy as a result of the long and costly conflict with Iraq.

With the end of the war in 1988, via a cease-fire that was itself a belated submission to pragmatism, and the death of Ayatollah Khomeini the following year, Iran's foreign policy began to shed some of its revolutionary radicalism. From this point onward, Iran's national interests increasingly appeared to trump ideological considerations in shaping its interaction with the world—with some notable exceptions. In the late 1990s, a domestically focused political reform movement made the case for the primacy of national interest in foreign policy decision making, with some notable successes in reining in the excesses of Iran's ideologues.

As the reformist strategy of managed change stumbled, however, the internal political landscape shifted yet again, and the ascendance of Ahmadinejad reoriented Iranian foreign policy toward a considerably harder line and revived the ideological themes of the revolution. "We cannot have a foreign policy without ideas," commented Said Jalili, foreign ministry official and close Ahmadinejad confidant, before his promotion to serve as Iran's chief nuclear negotiator. "There was a time when people were saying we have to eliminate ideology from our foreign policy. I never understood this."[17] In fact, Jalili spent much of his first one-on-one meeting with European Union (EU) foreign policy chief Javier Solana—a five-hour session—lecturing the EU official.

The impact of Ahmadinejad was felt sooner and more dramatically in Iran's foreign policy than its internal sphere through Iran's accelerating nuclear program; its emboldened regional posture and involvement with Hamas, Hezbollah, and Iraq; and, of course, the president's rancorous statements about Israel and the Holocaust. With their internal adversaries on the wane, Iranian hard-liners began asserting a newly reborn brashness and greater audacity on the international scene.

This approach reflects their innately Hobbesian worldview, a legacy of the revolutionary decade and the war with Iraq, and an aversion to compromise that is grounded in the conviction that acceding to international demands will be read as weakness and intensify pressure on the regime. As a columnist in a hard-line newspaper declared last year, "our world is not a fair one and everyone gets as much power as he can, not for his power of reason or the adaptation of his request to the international laws, but by his bullying."[18] Molded by their perception of an inherently hostile world and the conviction that the exigencies of regime survival justify its actions, Iranian leaders seek to exploit every opening, pursue multiple or contradictory agendas,

---

17. Said Jalili, interview by Morteza Qamari Vafa and Akram Sharifi, Fars News Agency, March 7, 2007, www.farsnews.com/newstext.php?nn=8512130522 (accessed May 9, 2008).
18. Mehdi Mohammadi, "The Meaning of Wisdom," *Keyhan*, February 4, 2007, www.kayhan-news.ir/851115/2.HTM#other200 (accessed May 9, 2008).

play various capitals against one another, and engage in pressure tactics—including the limited use of force—to advance their interests.

Iran's assertive foreign policy since Ahmadinejad's election also underscores the regime's perverse but compelling incentive to preserve the long-standing antagonism toward Washington, as it reinvigorates the hard-liners' domestic constituencies and justifies their extremist policies. Finally, for much of the Iranian leadership, the paradoxes of the regional context validate a more belligerent, forceful approach. High oil prices and American difficulties in stabilizing Iraq are offset by the proximity of the U.S. military; rising frictions with the United States, Europe, and many of their Sunni Arab neighbors; and the uncertainty about Washington's intentions and motivations.

But even since the hard-liners have consolidated control over all institutions and decision making, Iranian foreign policy is neither immutable nor monolithic. In fact, it is only since 2005 that Iran has finally abandoned one of its most fiercely guarded revolutionary shibboleths, the rejection of diplomatic dialogue with its old adversary Washington. Following an intensifying internal debate over the utility of direct contacts with Washington, Ayatollah Khamenei proclaimed in March 2006 that "there are no objections" to talks with Washington "if the Iranian officials think they can make the Americans clearly understand the issues pertaining to Iraq." He also cautioned, however, that "we do not support the talks, if they provide a venue for the bullying, aggressive, and deceptive side to impose its own views."[19] His announcement echoed calls by conservative MPs and Iranian power brokers such as Larijani and Rafsanjani and marked the first time in postrevolutionary history that the entire Iranian political spectrum, at the highest level, has publicly endorsed talks with the United States. Khamenei has reiterated his willingness to countenance a better relationship with Washington as recently as January 2008.

Moreover, it is clear that a critical mass within the Iranian political elite dissociate themselves from the stridency of the Ahmadinejad approach to foreign policy. The conservative-dominated parliament summoned his foreign minister for grilling over the president's denial of the Holocaust, and a number of U.S. officials have gone on record in late 2007 with praise for apparent Iranian cooperation in stemming the flow of roadside bombs to help U.S. efforts to stabilize Iraq. A more centrist Islamic Republic would most likely avoid some of the worst excesses of the Ahmadinejad era, and could over time develop a more constructive role vis-à-vis U.S. interests and allies in the region. Hassan Ruhani, the former chief nuclear negotiator who remains close to Rafsanjani, has been one of the most prominent and persis-

---

19. Ayatollah Ali Khamenei, speech in Mashhad on March 21, 2006, broadcast by the Vision of the Islamic Republic of Iran Network 1, World News Connection.

tent advocates of a more moderate international approach. In a November 2007 speech, he counseled that Iran "must act wisely in order to distance ourselves from tensions because these tensions in no way serve the interests of the country's economy, or indeed the interests of any political or economic aspect of the country. We should not give excuses to the enemies, and we should not provoke them with rash remarks."[20]

Still, in looking toward the future, it is important to note that a positive shift in Iran's internal politics—one that swings the pendulum back toward the center or even toward a more liberalized domestic order—will not necessarily facilitate new cooperation on the international front. The power struggle that dominated Iran during the reformist zenith complicated its decision making, and the exigencies of internal competition constrained even those leaders who might have been amenable from reaching out to Washington. Thus, after auspicious initial signals at the outset of Khatami's first term, the reformers refrained from overtures to the United States simply to avoid provoking hard-line reactions from their rivals. Moreover, shifts in Iran's internal politics may undermine whatever international consensus remains on Iran, which could stymie efforts to address the most problematic elements of Iran's foreign policy.

---

20. "Ruhani: Societies That Make Up Enemies Always Fail—Cannot Eliminate Rivals," *Farhang-e Ashti*, November 22, 2007, www.ashtidaily.com/detail.aspx?cid=119783 (accessed May 9, 2008).

2

Sources of Iranian Influence and Significance

In September 2004, the then-minister of defense of the Islamic Republic of Iran, Ali Shamkhani, was interviewed on the Qatar-based Al-Jazeera satellite television station. Shamkhani, whose ethnic background is Arab, spoke in Persian, and forcefully rebuffed the suggestion by his interviewer that Iran found itself pressured or encircled by the presence of the U.S. military along Iran's borders. "I say the presence of Americans is not a sign of strength," Shamkhani countered. "We are present from Quds to Kandahar. We are present in the Persian Gulf, Afghanistan, and Iraq."[1]

Shamkhani's boast has been echoed and augmented by his successors, particularly as Iran's hard-liners have recaptured control of its internal dynamics and the regional balance of power has shifted in its favor. "Who can deny Iran's political status and international respect?" Ayatollah Khamenei proclaimed in a September 2007 address to government officials. "Who can deny the influence of the government of the Islamic Republic today in the region's policies and even in extraregional policies? Who can deny the respect that the Islamic Republic enjoys among Muslim nations? Which country can claim that the head of the country, the country's senior officials, can go to another Muslim country and find that that country's Muslim people—even if their government doesn't want it—congregate and raise slogans in his support, other than the Islamic Republic? It is only the Islamic Republic whose leaders have spiritual, true, and political standing among other nations."[2] With the distinct exception of the United States, Iran today is unquestionably the leading power in the Persian Gulf and has succeeded in extending its sway to key constituencies across the Arab world by exploiting the shifts in regional dynamics to its own advantage.

Tehran's immodest claims and emboldened stance strike at the heart of the salience of Iran today, both to the broader Muslim world as well as with respect to U.S. strategic interests. By virtue of its history, its size, its intricate cultural and religious bonds, and the active efforts of a government whose

---

1. Barbara Slavin, "Iran Seeing Opportunities to Capitalize on Turmoil in Iraq," *USA Today*, September 14, 2004.
2. Ayatollah Ali Khamenei, speech to government officials in Tehran on September 22, 2007, broadcast on the Vision of the Islamic Republic of Iran Network 1, translated by BBC Monitoring.

legitimacy is steeped in the notion of its religious and regional primacy, Iran today lies at the heart of the many dilemmas that dominate the Islamic world and U.S. policy toward it. Indeed, senior U.S. officials have repeatedly described Iran as the central threat to American interests in the region—Secretary of State Condoleezza Rice called it the "most important single-country strategic challenge to the United States and to the kind of Middle East that we want to see."[3]

As American officials warn and Iranian officials trumpet, Iran has profound sway in the wider Islamic world precisely because its reach is felt with such force. Through its patronage of Hezbollah and other militants across the region, Iran is a vital player in any Arab-Israeli peace process and in the broader political order of the Levant and other corners of the Middle East. With the distinct exception of Washington, no capital has greater capacity to shape the future of the two key battlegrounds of the war on terror, Afghanistan and Iraq. With the world's second leading oil and gas reserves, Iran is flush with cash, insulating its government from the consequences of economic and political radicalism and enabling its leadership to subsidize its proxies and court new patrons. Iran's clout is also felt beyond its strategic and financial weight through the cultivation of a distinct model of Islamic politics that is propagated via media and example.

While Tehran has a variety of vehicles at its disposal for advancing its foreign policy, the purpose of this monograph is to analyze the sources of Iran's influence in the Islamic world. Rather than offer a comprehensive history of Iran's relations with each individual Muslim country, the following section seeks to identify the patterns and mechanisms of Iranian influence over the range of states that have predominantly Muslim populations as well as those, such as China and Russia, with sizeable or historically relevant Muslim minorities. By examining five broad dimensions of Iran's foreign policy, we can better appreciate Iran's relevance in the Islamic world, as well as the salience of religious identity for Tehran's worldview, and in turn identify ways that U.S. policy might respond more effectively to the multifaceted challenges posed by the Islamic Republic.

Long Reach

Although the mobilization of the revolution represented an intensely internal affair, the Islamic Republic from the outset defined itself in relation to external powers and issues, in particular Iran's historical relationship with the United States and the aspiration of its leaders to replicate the revolution across the Muslim umma. At the outset of the revolution, Khomeini viewed

---

3.   Secretary of State Condoleezza Rice, remarks made in press briefing en route to Egypt, July 30, 2007, www. state.gov/secretary/rm/2007/89836.htm (accessed April 15, 2008).

the need to extend Iran's revolutionary fervor as a fundamental prerequisite for the state's survival, arguing that "Islam does not regard various Islamic countries differently and is the supporter of all the oppressed peoples of the world. On the other hand, all the superpowers and the [great] powers have risen to destroy us. If we remain in an enclosed environment we shall definitely face defeat."[4]

At the outset of the revolution, Iran's salience to its fellow Muslim states stemmed from its explicit agenda of seeking to subvert its neighbors and promulgate its vision of an Islamic order. This enterprise encompassed the use of force and propaganda against its neighbors, direct aid to terrorist organizations, and threats against (as well as active assassinations of) individuals abroad deemed enemies of the Islamic Republic. All this activity was sanctioned at the outset of the revolution by the messianic worldview that pervaded Iran's clerical leadership, who eschewed nationalist distinctions in favor of appeals to the wider umma. "Terrorism was easily accepted and even congenial to revolutionaries; at a time when the regime was still not consolidated, terrorism was an extension of revolutionary politics: clandestine, coercive, and nonattributable."[5]

What began with sympathetic demonstrations of indigenous dissatisfaction among Shia communities in Kuwait, Bahrain, and Saudi Arabia evolved into a semiofficial Iranian administration dedicated to toppling the status quo in the broader Islamic world. Iran's internal divisions extended to, and exacerbated, its external adventures, with the Foreign Ministry, the Revolutionary Guards, and the Intelligence Ministry at various times establishing distinct organs intended to coordinate proxy revolutionary groups abroad and propagate Islamist propaganda sympathetic to Tehran. Through these instruments, Iran helped to incite an attempted coup in Bahrain in 1981, bombings in Kuwait targeting the U.S. Embassy and other American interests in 1983, an assassination attempt against Kuwait's emir in 1985, provocative anti-Saudi and anti-American rallies during the annual pilgrimage, and other subversive actions against its neighbors. After the Iraqi invasion in 1980, Iran's zeal in exporting its revolution inevitably became caught up with its war objectives and strategy, as the clerical regime undertook bombings of regional oil facilities and attacks against Kuwaiti and Saudi tankers.

Iran's early efforts deliberately aimed at destabilizing the leadership of its fellow Muslim states, many of which it considered illegitimate. Egypt— whose postrevolutionary relations with Iran were soured by President Sadat's welcome to the Shah and his decision to sign a peace treaty with

---

4.   R.K. Ramazani, *Revolutionary Iran Challenge and Response in the Middle East* (Baltimore: Johns Hopkins University Press, 1986), 24.

5.   Shahram Chubin, *Whither Iran? Reform, Domestic Politics and National Security* (London: International Institute for Strategic Studies, Adelphi Paper 342, 2002), 89.

Israel—regularly accused Iran of supporting and training members of the outlawed Islamic Group. Iran extended support to the Kurdistan Workers Party (PKK) and a variety of other religious and ethnically based opposition groups around the region to the persistent irritation of other regimes. During this heady period, Iran's revolutionary fervor extended far beyond its immediate neighborhood to the Philippines, Pakistan, and the Chinese province of Xinjiang.[6]

As a monarchy with close ties to the United States, potent claims to international Islamic leadership, and a vulnerable Shia minority, Saudi Arabia offered a particularly tempting target. Based on doctrinal differences and long political frictions, Khomeini himself appeared to harbor a particular loathing for Riyadh, writing in his will that "Muslims should curse tyrants, including the Saudi royal family, these traitors to God's great shrine, may God's curse and that of his prophets and angels be upon them."[7] In addition to using the hajj as incendiary political theater, Iran was implicated by Washington as having directed the 1996 bombing of the Khobar Towers in Dhahran, in which nineteen American servicemen were killed. The June 2001 U.S. indictment offers detailed allegations of the plot, arguing that it was perpetrated by a little-known group of Saudi Shia with the direct involvement and support of the group's Iranian patrons.[8] In response, Washington reportedly attempted to disrupt Iran's terrorist activities by exposing its intelligence officers abroad.[9]

Beyond its patronage of external proxies and cultivation of fifth-column clients within its Shia orbit, Tehran also invested assiduously in developing a network of like-minded state allies, providing military materiel and financial assistance to Sudan's Islamic government in exchange for the establishment of joint terrorist training camps in that country. In cooperation with its satellite organization, Hezbollah, which is considered in greater depth below, Iranian authorities are also alleged to have masterminded the 1994 bombing of a Jewish cultural center in Argentina that killed eighty-five people. A protracted Argentinean judicial process has alleged that the bombing was carried out by Hezbollah operatives on Tehran's direct order. In 2006, Argentina issued arrest warrants for several senior Iranian figures, including Rafsanjani, former foreign minister Ali Akbar Velayati, and former intelligence minister Ali Fallahian.[10] Throughout this same period, Iran also sponsored

6.   Graham E. Fuller, *The 'Center of the Universe': The Geopolitics of Iran* (Boulder, CO: Westview Press, 1991), 233; John W. Garver, *China and Iran: Ancient Partners in the Post-Imperial World* (Seattle: University of Washington Press, 2006), 131–8.

7.   Baqer Moin, *Khomeini: Life of the Ayatollah* (New York: St. Martin's Press, 1999), 305.

8.   James Risen and Jane Perlez, "Terror, Iran and the U.S.," *New York Times*, June 23, 2001.

9.   Barbara Slavin, "Officials: U.S. 'Outed' Iran's Spies in 1997," *USA Today*, March 29, 2004.

10.   Larry Rohter, "Argentine Judge Indicts Iranians in Bombing of Jewish Center," *New York Times*, March 10, 2003; Patrick J. McDonnell, "Argentina Issues Arrest Warrants," *Los Angeles Times*, November 10, 2006.

a prolonged assassination campaign directed against dissidents and prominent opponents of Islamic rule. Victims included Kurdish leader Abdulrahman Qasemlu in 1989, former Iranian prime minister Shahpour Bakhtiar in 1991, and several leaders of the Mojahideen-e Khalq organization, which is designated by the State Department as a foreign terrorist organization.

In this respect, it is critical to consider recent evidence of collusion between Iranian hard-liners and al-Qaida. The independent commission investigating the September 11 attacks found that a number of the hijackers had passed through Iran on their way to and from Afghanistan in the months preceding the attacks. While the commission found "no evidence that Iran or Hezbollah was aware of the planning for what later became the 9/11 attack," the report noted that the hijackers' transit of Iran was facilitated by the tacit assistance of Iranian officials, who agreed not to stamp al-Qaida members' passports as a means of enabling them to elude detection by their own governments.[11]

In the aftermath of the September 11 attacks and the U.S.-led military campaign to oust the Taliban in Afghanistan, al-Qaida operatives apparently continued to travel through Iran, and continued to plan terrorist operations from Iranian soil. Washington repeatedly accused Iran of providing safe haven to al-Qaida terrorists, including several prominent leaders such as Saad bin Laden, spokesman Suleiman Abu Ghaith, and security chief Saif al Adel. Related to these allegations are reports that Imad Mughniyeh, who headed Hezbollah's special operations directorate and topped the Bush Administration's most wanted terrorist list until his assassination in February 2008, also was supported by and harbored in Iran.

After intensifying public criticism by the U.S. government on this issue since early 2002, Iran confirmed that it has detained an unspecified number of individuals connected with al-Qaida, and later acknowledged that these included both "small and big-time elements."[12] The circumstances of their entry to Iran are not publicly known, nor are any details of their status beyond Iran's announced intention to put them on trial. Iran also claims to have deported at least five hundred individuals who fled Afghanistan on the heels of the U.S. military campaign. Although Iran has trumpeted these actions as evidence of its vigilance in countering al-Qaida's domestic and international threat, U.S. concerns about Iran's posture intensified after the May 2003 attacks on expatriate housing complexes in Saudi Arabia that were attributed to al-Qaida operatives, possibly working from Iran. As a result, Washington suspended the quiet constructive dialogue between the two governments that had developed after 9/11 on a limited range of regional issues.

---

11. *The 9/11 Commission Report: Final Report of the National Commission on Terrorist Attacks upon the United States* (Washington, DC: U.S. Government Printing Office, 2004), 241.

12. Douglas Jehl, "Iran Said to Hold Qaeda's No. 3, but to Resist Giving Him Up," *New York Times,* August 2, 2003.

These patterns of interaction contravene both the Islamic Republic's ac-commodating stance toward the 2001 U.S. military campaign in Afghani-stan and the well-established track record of hostility between Iran and al-Qaida's ascetic strand of Sunni militancy. This track record includes unremitting hostility between the Islamic Republic and the Taliban re-gime, which nearly escalated to direct military conflict in 1998. Specifi-cally with respect to al-Qaida, its ideology and worldview are unrelent-ingly opposed to the Shia branch of Islam, which its theologians brand as a heretical sect. Nonetheless, both al-Qaida's operational leadership and the radical hard-liners who dominate the senior ranks of Iran's security bureaucracy have demonstrated in the past a certain degree of doctrinal flexibility that has facilitated functional alliances irrespective of apparent ideological incompatibility.

Iran's eastern border is notoriously porous, as Iranian officials are prone to noting in their government's defense; however, even if true, Iran's opaque handling of its unwelcome guests strains credulity.[13] The substance of Iran's connections with al-Qaida is subject to innuendo and interpretation, like so many aspects of the terrorist threat. In the absence of any meaningful dia-logue or cooperation between Washington or its allies and Tehran on this specific issue, little progress can be made in resolving the issue. One plau-sible, although as yet unverified, explanation holds that Iran's reluctance to turn over captured al-Qaida operatives stems from concerns that such coop-eration could produce evidence of complicity between Iranian hard-liners and individual terrorists. Behind the scenes, Iranian officials have suggested exchanging its al-Qaida detainees for members of the Mojahideen-e Khalq organization being held by U.S. occupying forces in Iraq. Like many other episodes in the history of its turbulent relationship with Washington, Iran's insistence on clinging to what it perceives to be a valuable bargaining chip may lead to an overestimation of its potential leverage and an ultimate weak-ening of its own security.

Within this long history of radical Islamist agitation, Iranian involve-ment with two specific organizations—Lebanese Hezbollah and the Su-preme Council for the Islamic Revolution in Iraq (SCIRI, later renamed the Supreme Iraqi Islamic Council, SIIC)—stands out because of the direct Iranian role in their establishment and their ongoing organic connections with Tehran. SCIRI will be addressed in the subsequent section on Iran's involvement with zones of conflict. The role of Hezbollah remains one of the most complex and problematic legacies of Iran's efforts to spread its

---

13. Kenneth Pollack, *The Persian Puzzle: The Conflict between Iran and America* (New York: Random House, 2004), 358. As Pollack succinctly puts it, "Al-Qaeda is a savage group that had fought Iran up until just months beforehand, and that alone should have been enough for the Iranians to kill or imprison them. Thus, at some level their freedom had to have been intentional."

Islamic revolutionary fervor. Iranian officials helped to found the group, which was born of the fragments of a Shia militia and was crystallized by the 1982 Israeli invasion of Lebanon. An outgrowth of the intricate religious and familial ties among the region's Shia clerical establishment, Hezbollah today has both military and political arms, but remains closely associated with Iran's clerical leadership and has been called "the flagship of the Iranian revolution abroad."[14]

Hezbollah's track record as one of the world's foremost terrorist organizations is indisputable; until 9/11, its 1983 attack on barracks housing U.S. Marines in Lebanon constituted the largest loss of U.S. lives to a terrorist attack. As a result of this attack and several other devastating suicide bombings carried out by Hezbollah operatives during that period, Deputy Secretary of State Richard Armitage characterized the U.S. stance toward Hezbollah in late 2002 as a "blood debt," adding, "We're not going to forget it. . . . We're going to go after these problems just like a high school wrestler goes after a match: We're going to take them down one at a time."[15] In the 1980s, Hezbollah was responsible for aircraft hijackings as well as kidnappings of Americans and other Westerners, in addition to its reported involvement in two bombings in Argentina and other terrorist acts.

Despite this history, it would be inaccurate to view Hezbollah as a purely terrorist organization in the vein of al-Qaida. It has gradually evolved into something beyond a compliant Iranian surrogate. Although its leaders pay homage to Iran's supreme leader as their spiritual guide, the organization has publicly distanced itself from its early objective of establishing an Islamic state in Lebanon.[16] Through its long-standing provision of social services to the historically disenfranchised Lebanese Shia population, Hezbollah has made itself an indispensable part of the country's social fabric. Its role in forcing Israel's 2000 withdrawal from southern Lebanon won Hezbollah widespread acclaim in the region and gave it a potent mantle of popular legitimacy at home. For fifteen years, Hezbollah has also played a significant role in the Lebanese political system, where it now holds fourteen seats in the parliament and two cabinet portfolios.

However, neither Hezbollah nor its Iranian benefactors have yet suggested that they are prepared to see the organization make a wholesale transition away from its militant roots, and they rallied around the issue of the disputed Sheba Farms near the Lebanese-Israeli border as a pretext

---

14. David Menashri, *Post-Revolutionary Politics in Iran Religion,* Society and Power (London: Frank Cass, 2001), 247.

15. "Conditions Underlying Conflict Must Be Addressed, Armitage Says," U.S. Mission to the European Union, September 5, 2002, www.useu.be/Terrorism/USResponse/Sept0502ArmitageConflictIraqTerrorism.html (accessed April 16, 2008).

16. Augustus Richard Norton, *Hezbollah*: A *Short History* (Princeton, NJ: Princeton University Press, 2007), 46.

for maintaining its role as a "resistance" organization. Tehran continues to provide Hezbollah with substantial financial support, weaponry, and training, facilitated by its sole Arab ally, Syria, which uses its place in Hezbollah's supply chain to maintain substantial influence in Lebanon. The entrenchment of a triumphal, armed nonstate actor on the Lebanese political scene provokes anxiety for a number of domestic and regional actors, and the 2005 assassination of former Lebanese prime minister Rafiq Hariri made the situation even more volatile.

Within Lebanon, Hariri's death briefly appeared to create a turning point for Lebanon to become a more "normal" state and rid itself of the legacy of sectarian civil war and dueling foreign occupations. The Syrians were forced to withdraw their remaining thirty thousand troops, and the international community—with the support of an anti-Syrian majority in Lebanon's parliament elected in 2005—mobilized to press for Hezbollah's disarmament as well as for a UN inquiry into Syria's reported involvement in Hariri's murder and other political assassinations in Lebanon. The Bush administration trumpeted this "Cedar Revolution" as evidence of the success of its "Freedom Agenda" in bringing democracy to the Middle East. Such a shift would have significantly constrained one of Tehran's most valuable allies. As analyst Graham Fuller explained, "Iran has enjoyed unusual entrée and freedom in Lebanon mainly due to the collapse of local government authority. Any restitution of Lebanese central government authority will inevitably begin to circumscribe Iran's freestyle politicking in Lebanon."[17] Instead, Lebanon's long-established dynamics of political gridlock produced little change and made it clear that there was little prospect of any short-term demobilization of Hezbollah.

The ground shifted again in July 2006 after Hezbollah launched a provocative cross-border attack, killing three Israeli soldiers and seizing two others. Israel responded with overwhelming force, including a naval blockade, massive air strikes, and the dispatch of ground troops into southern Lebanon. Once again, this episode initially appeared to undermine Iran and its longstanding client in Lebanon, as several key Arab states immediately criticized Hezbollah while Washington made clear that the United States was prepared to see the Israelis do the maximum damage to Hezbollah's position. Briefly, at least, the clash in Lebanon invoked the specter of a wider regional war or possible Israeli action against Syria that might jeopardize the value of the alliance for Tehran.

However, over the course of the 34-day conflict, regional popular opinion mobilized behind Hezbollah, which proved surprisingly capable of withstanding Israel's bombardment. Its self-declared mantle of resistance was now embraced by Arabs across the region, and its leader, Sayyid Hassan

---

17. Fuller, *The 'Center of the Universe,'* 131.

Nasrallah, attained cult hero status for his defiance, as did Ahmadinejad. Ultimately, the summer war represented a strategic bonanza for Iran, boosting its standing among the region's public and deferring any prospect that a coherent Lebanese government would emerge capable of disarming its Lebanese proxy. A year after the war, Iran claimed to have spent $155 million for reconstruction activities in Lebanon—moving more quickly and in some respects more effectively with direct assistance to its constituency than those external actors, such as the United States and Saudi Arabia, that provided even greater sums to the Lebanese government.[18] "The Iranian view at this moment is that they are on a winning streak," scholar Ali Ansari commented in September 2006. "They feel they've done it themselves, and in fact they haven't—they've just been the beneficiaries of pretty incoherent policies from Washington."[19]

Still, the picture was not as rosy as Ahmadinejad and his allies often depicted. Just as it strengthened Iran's image among the region's radicalized publics, the war, and the rising popular appeal of Nasrallah and Ahmadinejad, also exacerbated tensions between Iran and its powerful Arab neighbors, including Egypt and Saudi Arabia. In particular, the episode only cemented the view among Arab leaders that Iran represented a multifaceted threat to the regional order and generated renewed commitment in some capitals to trying to roll back Iran's influence. "Iran has become more dangerous than Israel itself," a Saudi newspaper editor told the *New York Times* in December 2006. "The Iranian revolution has come to renew the Persian presence in the region. This is the real clash of civilizations."[20]

Regional trepidations about Iranian influence in the Levant were exacerbated by Tehran's success in further insinuating itself into the Palestinian arena. Historically, Hezbollah had served as the mechanism for Iranian efforts to develop linkages with (Sunni) Palestinian militant groups, including the Popular Front for the Liberation of Palestine-General Command, Hamas, and Palestinian Islamic Jihad. Obviously, Israel and the Palestinians have always loomed large in the worldview of the Islamic Republic, and the use of anti-Israeli rhetoric will be considered below as part of the discussion about Iran's cultural influence across the Muslim world. However, with respect to its support for pan-Islamic revolution, the Holy Land represented a special complication for the Islamic Republic. Some Iran revolutionaries had historic ties to the Popular Front for the Liberation of Palestine, but for the most part

---

18. Raed Rafei and Borzou Daragahi, "Iran Builds a Presence in Lebanon," *Los Angeles Times*, August 17, 2007.

19. Scott Peterson, "Why Iran Sees No Rush for a Nuke Deal," *Christian Science Monitor*, September 7, 2006, www.csmonitor.com/2006/0907/p06s02-wome.html (accessed April 15, 2008).

20. Hassan M. Fattah, "Bickering Saudis Struggle for an Answer to Iran's Rising Influence in the Middle East," *New York Times*, December 22, 2006.

revolutionary Iran's relationship to Palestinian leaders during its early years was fractious as a result of cultural differences and the spillover from Iran's involvement in Lebanon.[21]

Eventually, Yasser Arafat's decision to align with Saddam after the Iraqi invasion of Iran in 1980 and his later participation in the U.S.-brokered peace process created lasting animosity between the Islamic Republic and the most prominent representative of the Palestinian people, forcing Tehran to channel its support to alternative organizations. Even here, Iran was limited by the apparent discomfort of the Palestinian Islamist groups with getting too close to a Shia patron, eventually finding some success by working through Hezbollah to facilitate operational linkages. Reports cite estimates as high as $100 million in Iranian funding to individual organizations, but Palestinian militants dispute these assertions, claiming that Iranian aid is philanthropic in nature and of a much lesser magnitude.

Iran rejects U.S. criticism of its involvement with Hezbollah and Palestinian militants; its official justifications differentiate between terrorist activities and what Tehran characterizes as legitimate resistance against occupation. This paradoxical position has generated occasional evidence that some elements of the Iranian power structure could be persuaded to countenance an eventual peace agreement between the Palestinians and Israel. The Foreign Ministry declared as recently as October 2002 that Iran would not stand in the way of a final, two-state solution—a position that former president Khatami reiterated again publicly in 2006[22]—and half-heartedly accepted (at least in its official dialogue with Saudi Arabia) the Saudi-initiated Arab Peace Initiative. Equally important, Iranian policymakers have recognized the risk that Iran's assistance to militants opposing the Middle East peace process could drag the country directly into conflict, particularly in the post-9/11 environment of preemption as a tool of counterterrorism.

Still, the Iranian leadership's adherence to extremist rhetoric and close association with rejectionist groups ultimately limits the government's flexibility on this issue. Having entrenched its opposition to Israel so prominently and absolutely, Tehran has gradually found itself in the complicated position of being more unyielding than the Palestinians themselves. Since the outset of the second Palestinian intifada in September 2000, the few official voices of moderation have been increasingly drowned out by Iranian radicals, and the failure of the Clinton administration's bid to resolve the conflict reenergized Iranian opposition. In January 2002, a ship laden with fifty tons of Iranian weapons and explosives destined for the Palestinian Authority (PA)

---

21. Trita Parsi, *Treacherous Alliance: The Secret Dealings of Israel, Iran and the United States* (New Haven, CT: Yale University Press, 2007), 82–86.

22. "Khatami Says Iran Would Accept Two-State Solution," Radio Free Europe/Radio Liberty, September 5, 2006, www.rferl.org/featuresarticle/2006/09/9d08fc7e-4903-4e4c-a592-4818e4cbd47b.html (accessed April 15, 2008).

was discovered off the coast of Israel, with its captain claiming that its cargo was loaded in Iran. Iran has also continued to host an annual conclave on the Palestinian intifada, or uprising, which draws a veritable pantheon of terrorist leaders involved in violence against Israel.

The victory of the Palestinian Islamic movement Hamas in January 2006 parliamentary elections created a new opening for Iran's involvement in this arena. The elections were the product of U.S. pressure to create a legitimate post-Arafat government that might be capable of negotiating with the Israelis, but the outcome shocked the West and dramatically fractured the relationship between the PA and its primary external backers, Europe and the United States. The Quartet—composed of the United States, Russia, the European Union, and the United Nations—reacted swiftly, praising the conduct of the elections themselves but conditioning any further assistance on Hamas's fulfillment of three basic principles—commitment to nonviolence, recognition of Israel, and acceptance of previous agreements signed by the PA. The predictable refusal of Hamas to accept these conditions sparked an economic crisis for the Palestinians but a golden opportunity for Tehran to buy access and leverage with one of the more historically independent Palestinian organizations and to burnish its credentials as a defender of Muslim causes. Iran quickly offered Hamas $50 million in assistance, showered its leadership with VIP treatment, and reportedly began providing long-term training assistance to the organization's militia.[23]

As with the 2006 summer war in Lebanon, Iran's successful exploitation of the Palestinian predicament after the Hamas parliamentary victory rankled its Arab neighbors. The leading Arab states felt themselves bound by their relationship with Washington—as well as their own investment in the 2002 Arab Peace Initiative and their antipathy toward any movement with roots in the Muslim Brotherhood—to adhere to the Western line on isolating the Hamas-led government. However, as the standoff between Hamas and the West endured, some Arab representatives also grumbled privately about ceding yet another piece of critical political turf in the heart of the Arab world to Tehran. A desire to remain engaged with Hamas and relevant in an Islamist conflict no doubt inspired Saudi efforts to broker a Palestinian national unity government in early 2007.

For Washington, the insertion of Iran into a much more significant role in intra-Palestinian politics generated a different set of concerns. Together with Iran's consolidated position in Lebanon via Hezbollah and its preponderant position in Iraq, the Iranian embrace of Hamas helped create a widely shared fear of revived revolutionary meddling by Iran. In response, the United States tried to build an anti-Iranian alliance in the region that would be anchored

---

23.   Gideon Alon, "Shin Bet Director: Hundreds of Hamas Men Being Trained in Iran," *Haaretz*, March 13, 2007.

by a new push by the Bush administration to broker an Israeli-Palestinian peace accord. The broader elements of this strategy will be considered below in the discussion of the "Shia crescent," but with respect to the peace process, the tangible effects of this purported new entente were modest, involving a splashy peace "conference" in November 2007 that produced little more than a photo opportunity. Arab leaders, relieved to see belated U.S. attention to the Palestinian cause, participated in the conference warily, but the Saudis and Egyptians also renewed their efforts to reunite the warring Palestinian factions. For their part, Iranian leaders denounced the whole affair as a sham. "It is clear that this is a conspiracy against the Palestinians," Ayatollah Khamenei declared in October 2007. "Some of the governments of the region used to say in past years: We are not more Palestinian than the Palestinians. . . . Very well, don't be more Palestinian than the Palestinians. Now the Palestinians themselves are saying, 'We don't accept this peace conference.' They call it a ploy and a ruse."[24]

Given the intense concerns in the region and in Washington about Iran's embrace of a pan-Islamic vision and its efforts to destabilize other Muslim states, it is important to note several central caveats in the context of this discussion. First, an objective review of Iranian foreign policy makes clear that revolutionary Islamism has never served as the single or even the central catalyst of Iran's international approach. Even during its most radical period, the Islamic Republic's engagement with the world was shaped by a variety of factors and motivations, including a deeply engrained nationalist imperative, an entrenched resentment of the machinations of world powers, and a legitimate recognition of the state's inherent strategic insecurity.[25]

As a result, Iran's efforts to extend its Islamic Republic to the broader Muslim world have been inconsistent and subject to the prerequisites of other interests and incentives. Ideological dexterity and a keen appreciation of the relative interests at stake generated relative reticence from Tehran in conflicts such as Chechnya and Xinjiang, where great power repression of Muslim populations might have been expected to produce active assistance from the self-proclaimed leader of the Islamic world.[26] However, in both cases, the strategic and economic benefits of a constructive relationship with Moscow and Beijing were too valuable to Tehran to risk for the uncertain gains of assisting its coreligionists.

In April 1997, just one month prior to Iran's surprising presidential election, a German court ruled that Iranian officials ordered the 1992 assassina-

---

24. Ayatollah Ali Khamenei, speech in Tehran, broadcast on Voice of the Islamic Republic of Iran Radio 1 on October 14, 2007, World News Connection.

25. For more on the sources of Iran's foreign policy, see Suzanne Maloney, "Identity and Change in Iran's Foreign Policy," in *Identity and Foreign Policy in the Middle East*, eds. Shibley Telhami and Michael Barnett (Ithaca, NY: Cornell University Press, 2002), 88–116.

26. On the evolution of Iran's stance toward Xinjiang, see Garver, *China and Iran*, 131–38.

tion of three Kurdish dissident leaders and their translator at the Mykonos restaurant in Berlin. While the court declined to name the officials personally, it attributed the murders to a government committee that comprised the supreme leader, the president, the intelligence minister, and other security officials. The verdict roiled Iran's relations with Germany and other European states, and the implications helped the new reformist leadership to persuade the government to curtail its excesses in one small but significant fashion, by ending the practice of dissident assassinations abroad. This episode highlights the interconnections between Iranian domestic and foreign policy. Over time, Tehran's export of the revolution became largely the province of two state organizations over which the elected government had only marginal control: the Intelligence Ministry and the Revolutionary Guards. The reformists' efforts to reshape the Intelligence Ministry succeeded only later, after the revelation of the ministry's involvement in the murders of four Iranian writers and dissidents in 1998; moreover, the modest efforts to create a new culture of accountability within the ministry reportedly have been rolled back under Ahmadinejad.

The Mykonos verdict also contributed to the changing decision-making climate within Iran that enabled Tehran in May 1999 to finally rid itself of its official attachment to the 1989 fatwa by Ayatollah Khomeini sentencing British-Indian writer Salman Rushdie to death. The Khatami administration did not, in fact, depart from the long-standing position of the Iranian government that it could not retract the Rushdie fatwa, but it indicated that the government itself would not seek its implementation. This paved the way for the two countries to resume full diplomatic relations at the ambassadorial level after ten years. The difference came largely in the context; Khatami's broader transformation of the prevailing discourse from Tehran "carefully prepared the ground" and ensured that Tehran's subtle dissociation from this sticking point would be received with greater credibility.[27]

Even in its own neighborhood, where exporting the revolution arguably coincided with Iran's security interests in friendly regimes, the war with Iraq and the economic devastation left in its wake proved to be powerful stimulants for a revised approach. The same social, political, and economic dynamics that shaped the reformist rethinking of Iran's domestic policies clearly helped persuade Tehran of the need for greater restraint in its agitation abroad. President Khatami explicitly embarked on an effort to "reduce tensions" with Saudi Arabia and the other Persian Gulf littoral states, and he largely succeeded in that effort. In addition to economic incentives, a central component of Tehran's new relationship with the Gulf was the initiation of bilateral security dialogues with Saudi Arabia, Kuwait, and other

27.   Ali M. Ansari, *Iran, Islam and Democracy: The Politics of Managing Change* (London: The Royal Institute for International Affairs, 2000), 140.

governments. As the discussion on the Shia crescent below will detail, this rapprochement has survived the rocky Ahmadinejad years with greater continuity than many in Washington would presume.

Finally, it is also important to recognize that Iran's policies have facilitated a utilitarian propensity among regional leaders to attribute the causes and implementation of domestic instability to the conveniently hostile Islamic Republic. This is not to minimize in any way Iran's role in supporting violent groups and attempting to undermine its neighbors and rivals in the Islamic world. Still, for those Gulf states with significant Shia minorities—Bahrain, Kuwait, and Saudi Arabia—the events of 1979 created new causes for activism and alienation within those minority populations and for misgivings by their governments. "Indeed, whenever there have been disturbances by Gulf Shias, all the blame has been laid on Tehran's doorstep, and there has been little willingness to admit that Shias in several countries have real grievances."[28]

Role in Zones of Conflict: The Rise of the Shia

Iran's experience in exporting its revolution has been decidedly mixed. Ironically, the places where Tehran today wields the greatest clout are the states in which U.S. military intervention eliminated Iran's long-standing adversaries. While Iran's fortunes in Washington have ebbed and flowed over the past three years, the context for its regional interests and influence has been permanently and affirmatively altered as a direct result of the two recent U.S. military campaigns. Indeed, Iran appears to be the chief beneficiary of the U.S.-effected change of power in Baghdad and Kabul. Owing to its direct ethnic and religious ties to the populations of both countries, Iran has always had intense and very particular interests in both Iraq and Afghanistan, and, as a result of American actions, finds itself with enhanced access and vastly greater leverage in both countries. Indeed, Iran's position in Iraq has been strengthened so dramatically by the U.S. intervention that some pundits actually suggested that Tehran might have "lured" Washington into invading.[29]

Prior to September 11, 2001, Afghanistan had emerged gradually as a serious but mostly low-level threat to Tehran. Beginning in the mid-1990s, officials of the Islamic Republic viewed the advance of the Taliban to be a direct and immediate threat to their rule on both a strategic and ideological level. As an unknown movement with direct links to the Pakistani intelligence services,

---

28. Shireen Hunter, "Outlook for Iranian-Gulf Relations: Greater Cooperation or Renewed Risk of Conflict?" in *Iran, Iraq, and the Arab Gulf States,* ed. Joseph A. Kechichian (New York: Palgrave, 2001), 435.
29. Ted Galen Carpenter, "Did Iran Lure U.S. into Iraq?" United Press International, June 9, 2004.

the Taliban were perceived by Tehran as an inherently untrustworthy group; their barbarous treatment of Shia Afghans—whom the Taliban deemed apostates—very nearly drew the two countries into direct conflict. In addition, at some very basic level, the Taliban's ideological pretensions rankled Iran's more sophisticated, traditionally schooled clergy and appealed to the basic prejudices toward tribalism that many Iranians embrace. Foreign Minister Kamal Kharrazi dismissed the group as "a disgrace to Islam," and even Iran's hard-line clergy dissociated themselves from the cultural nihilism that reigned in Afghanistan.[30] "Taliban" quickly became shorthand for uneducated, crude, and reactionary—a meaning that is still somewhat operative, judging from the rhetoric of Iran's 2005 presidential campaign.[31]

Beyond their cultural affront, however, the Taliban came disturbingly close to direct conflict with the Iranian regime. In 1998, the Islamic Republic massed hundreds of thousands of troops along its eastern border in hastily organized war games in response to the killing of eight Iranian diplomats and a journalist during the Taliban takeover of the city of Mazar-e Sharif. More generally, the Taliban's tolerance of poppy growing aggravated the problem of drug use and smuggling in and through Iran, and contributed to the gradual erosion of Iran's eastern border security. Ironically, as a result of the ambivalent reaction that the Taliban's rise drew from Washington as well as its quixotic attempts to lure Western energy companies, Tehran viewed the group as a stalking horse of American influence. As a result of these challenges, Tehran continued to funnel resources to the primary remaining Afghan opposition movement, the Northern Alliance, while participating in the "Six plus Two" conflict resolution process along with the United States, Russia, and Afghanistan's other neighbors.

Iran's support for the Northern Alliance and its track record of involvement with international efforts to defuse Afghanistan's internal conflicts positioned Tehran to play a key role in the events that unfolded in the aftermath of the September 11 attacks. At least at the outset of the U.S.-led military campaign, Iran's interests in Afghanistan dovetailed neatly with Washington's, and its close ties to the Northern Alliance and operational history on the ground in Afghanistan helped Tehran provide meaningful assistance to the effort. Nominally, Iran's leadership opposed the U.S. strikes on the Taliban, but in practice the Iranians "were so enthusiastic that they just about offered to do the planning" and facilitated unprecedented cooperation with the U.S. military in support of the campaign.[32] Tehran also played an essential and

---

30. Elaine Sciolino, "Iran Finds a Not-So-Great Satan on Its Doorstep," *New York Times*, September 20, 1998.

31. During the second round of the campaign, opponents of hard-liner Mahmoud Ahmadinejad circulated text messages to potential voters comparing the former mayor of Tehran to the Taliban.

32. Pollack, *The Persian Puzzle*, 346.

constructive role in the immediate post-conflict stabilization and reconstruction of Afghanistan, culminating with the November 2001 Bonn conference
that established an interim government in Afghanistan as well as a political process for a permanently elected administration. At the initial pledging
conferences to provide international assistance to the new government in
Kabul, Iran was the lead donor, offering an additional $100 million at a fol-
low-up event in 2006.[33] The congruence of American and Iranian interests
in Afghanistan helped sustain a constructive mid-level dialogue between
the two governments until May 2003—the first such direct and officially acknowledged talks since the conclusion of the hostage crisis.

Since the fall of the Taliban, Tehran has remained a critical player in Afghanistan, although the level of trust and cooperation with the United States
has declined significantly. While on an official level the Islamic Republic continues to back the democratically elected government of Afghan President
Hamid Karzai, Iran also moved quickly after the ouster of the Taliban to cultivate multiple avenues of influence in the postwar power vacuum. Iranian
exports to Afghanistan doubled between 2003 and 2006, and its investment
in major infrastructure projects, such as the construction of a 125-mile highway to Herat and improvements to the railway system, has had a multiplier
effect by facilitating increased trade flows along the improved transportation
corridors and into South and Central Asian markets.[34]

However, Iranian involvement has also come to encompass considerable infusions of resources and intelligence operatives and the promotion
of close ties with a range of Afghan political figures and warlords, some of
whom are inherently inimical to the stability of the new Afghan government. Most recently, according to Washington, Iran's efforts to exert influence in Afghanistan have included direct financial and military support
to a revived amalgamation of its old adversary, the Taliban. These policies
reflect a desire to counter Washington's continuing military and political
involvement in Afghanistan, as well as a combination of opportunism and
hedging on the part of hard-liners within the Iranian government, who are
presumably eager to assert themselves in what they perceive to be their
natural sphere of influence.

The Iranian approach to Iraq and the U.S.-led military campaign there
presents many parallels to Afghanistan, but on a much more dramatic and
significant scale. Iranian officials harbored deeply seated and long-standing
grievances with Saddam Hussein, but as with Afghanistan, they publicly
opposed Washington's decision to unseat him while playing a modest but

---

33. Mohsen M. Milani, "Iran's Policy Towards Afghanistan," *Middle East Journal* 60, no. 2
    (Spring 2006).
34. Ibid.; Marc Sappenfield, "Afghan Business Thrives on Iran's Border," *Christian Science
    Monitor*, August 10, 2007, www.csmonitor.com/2007/0810/p01s08-wosc.html (accessed
    April 15, 2008).

generally constructive supporting role during the initial conflict. Again, like the Afghan case, Tehran had nurtured intimate and enduring ties with the primary external opposition groups to Saddam, as well as to the Kurds, and after the collapse of the regime, backed their direct participation in the U.S.-led process of reconstituting an Iraqi government. With the distance of several years, these Iranian decisions are justified by their success. Still, it is worth noting that given the antagonism and mistrust between Washington and Tehran, the cooperation of Iran and its various proxies and allies in Iraq was by no means assured at the time, and in fact proved critical to averting a variety of early disasters for U.S. policy in Iraq.[35]

In the immediate aftermath of the U.S.-led toppling of Saddam Hussein's regime, Iranian and American interests were in fact somewhat congruent. Though their definitions and timelines certainly differed, at the outset both Tehran and Washington sought a democratic government in Baghdad under the sovereign authority of Iraqis. From official statements and anecdotal evidence, it does not appear that Iran viewed post-Saddam Iraq as especially ripe for the export of the particularly Khomeinist model of Islamist state organized around the principle of direct clerical rule. "They have their own different conditions, which is very different from Iranian case," Kamal Kharrazi, then serving as Iran's foreign minister, acknowledged to an American interviewer in May 2005. "If this model has been applicable in Iran, it does not mean necessarily that it would be exactly applicable to other countries, including Iraq."[36]

Rather, Tehran appeared to be satisfied that an Iraqi democracy would generate a Shia-dominated leadership that would have the added advantage of long-standing relationships with its own Islamic leadership as a result of its sponsorship of various Iraqi opposition groups. But as the situation within Iraq deteriorated, and U.S. pressure on its nuclear activities intensified, Iran's interests in its neighbor evolved as well. Violence and uncertainty in Iraq has mitigated Iranian fears—relatively intense in early 2003—that the United States might exploit its military presence along Iran's borders to launch military strikes on Iran's nuclear facilities and/or implement regime change in a second member of the "axis of evil" troika. A certain amount of upheaval in Iraq benefits Iran by keeping U.S. troops bogged down and averting the possibility of an Iraqi resurgence—whether political, military, or economic—that might challenge Iranian hegemony as the predominant *regional* power in the Gulf. Of course, Iraqi instability would have an array of negative implications for Iran's security inter-

---

35. As Pollack notes, "If the Iranians had wanted to cause chaos in Iraq, they could have easily done so in the darkest days after the war, and the United States was fortunate that they did not." Pollack, *The Persian Puzzle*, 355.

36. Kamal Kharrazi, interview by Charlie Rose, *Charlie Rose Show*, PBS, May 4, 2005.

ests. This instability risks undermining the authority and legitimacy of its Iraqi allies, disproportionately targeting Shia coreligionists, and raising the specter of intensified ethnic and sectarian tensions within its own borders. Pursuing its own advantages while navigating the many risks appears to have engendered a multifaceted Iranian quest for influence in Iraq that is at times contradictory but to date has been largely successful.

On an official level, Iran has maintained a proactive and generally constructive posture. In August 2003, it was the first state to send an official delegation for talks with the Iraqi Governing Council, despite the fact that that body was largely handpicked by the United States. Iran has also dutifully participated in regular confabs organized for Iraq's neighbors and donors; earmarked financial support and export credits for Iraq; and engaged with Baghdad on specific assistance to key sectors, such as energy infrastructure and electrical power generation. Indeed, this formal relationship was only strengthened by the January 2005 elections that established a Shia-led interim administration. The new government's prime minister, Ibrahim Al Jafari, was a Shia who spent nearly a decade in exile in Iran, and shortly after assuming office he led a large delegation of Iraqi cabinet officials to Tehran, where he discussed border security, oil swaps, and Iran's announcement of $1 billion in assistance and loan guarantees. While in Iran, Jafari also took the opportunity to lay a wreath at the tomb of Ayatollah Khomeini. Jafari's trip followed only a week after a visit to Tehran by the Iraqi defense minister, who signed a memorandum of understanding for security cooperation and formally apologized to Iranians for the war crimes committed by Saddam's regime.

Jafari's close relationship with Tehran helped seal his fate. After Iraq's first parliamentary elections in December 2006, U.S. unhappiness over his intimacy with Iranian officials was one of several factors that cost Jafari his position. Ambassador Zalmay Khalilzad, then the U.S. envoy to Iraq, portrayed the decision by the Shia coalition not to reappoint Jafari as a victory for U.S. policy and a signal that Baghdad was distancing itself from Tehran. The decision "showed great courage on the part of key Shia leaders. . . . It showed that Sistani doesn't take Iranian direction. It showed that [SCIRI leader] Abdul Aziz Hakim doesn't succumb to Iranian pressure. He stood up to Iran. It showed the same thing about the Kurdish leaders."[37] But this expectation was to prove short-lived, as Prime Minister Nouri Al Maliki has maintained or even deepened post-Saddam Iraq's close association with the Islamic Republic.

Iran today has a wide-ranging economic relationship with the new Iraq, including billions of dollars in agreements with the Iraqi government for

---

37. David Ignatius, "In Iraq's Choice, a Chance for Unity," *Washington Post,* April 26, 2006, www.washingtonpost.com/wp-dyn/content/article/2006/04/25/AR2006042501650.html (accessed April 15, 2008).

future investments in the power sector, two oil pipelines from Basra to Abadan, and other infrastructure projects. Trade between the two countries reached $2 billion in 2006, according to Iran's envoy in Baghdad, nearly all of it Iranian exports to its neighbor.[38] Iran exports a panoply of consumer goods, from cars to air conditioners, into southern Iraq and Kurdistan, and tens of thousands of Iranian tourists flock to the Shia shrines in Najaf and Karbala each month.[39] The burgeoning economic relationship is to some extent a function of the close political ties and the security constraints for Western companies seeking access to Iraqi markets. However, it also reflects a deliberate effort by some Iraqi officials to focus on the country's "natural trading partners" in Turkey, Iran, and the Gulf, as well as the advantages of Iran's long experience in Iraq and comingled populations.[40]

Iranians and Iraqis endorse this official amity as a sign of political progress and maturity, and a welcome development for a region riven by three wars in the last thirty years, each of which involved Iraq. The newly cozy relations between Tehran and Baghdad can be interpreted to reflect pure self-interest on the part of both leaderships. "Iran doesn't want to see a turbulent atmosphere in Iraq," explained former Iranian deputy foreign minister Abbas Maleki. "It doesn't help Iranian national interests. If your neighbor's house is on fire, it means that your home is also in danger."[41] For their part, many Iraqis defend their acceptance of assistance from their former adversary and reject the implication that doing so makes them pawns of a foreign government. "There are many Iraqis like me," noted Fouad Kadim Douraqi, head of Karbala's Dawa Party. "We appreciate what they have offered us, but we don't allow them to do anything on our land or take positions on our behalf."[42]

However, as wide-ranging and multifaceted as it is, this formal cooperation represents only the tip of the iceberg with respect to Iran's involvement in post-Saddam Iraq. Much as they had done in post-conflict Afghanistan, the Iranians moved quickly and assiduously into Iraq in May 2003 to establish and exercise multiple avenues of influence, cultivating a network of intelligence agents and supporting a wide range of proxies and allies, among

38. "Iraq-Iran 2006 Trade Volume Exceeded $2b," *Tehran Times*, August 16, 2007, http://62.193.18.228/index_View.asp?code=150523 (accessed April 15, 2008); notably, the Iraqi finance minister suggests a figure only half as large. Sam Dagher, "Iran's Growing Presence in Iraq," *Christian Science Monitor*, July 25, 2007.

39. James Glanz, "Iraqi Contracts With Iran and China Concern U.S.," *New York Times*, October 18, 2007; Edward Wong, "Crippled, Iraq Leans on Longtime Enemy Iran for Trade," *International Herald Tribune*, March 13, 2007, www.iht.com/articles/2007/03/13/news/baghdad.php (accessed April 15, 2008).

40. Ali A. Allawi, *The Occupation of Iraq* (New Haven: Yale University Press, 2007), 312–13.

41. Borzou Daragahi, "Iran Views Neighboring Unrest with Alarm, Glee," *Daily Star* (Beirut), April 9, 2004.

42. Meghan K. Stack, "Iran's Internal Divisions Play Out in Iraqi Arena," *Los Angeles Times*, August 12, 2004.

them the radical Moqtada al Sadr and other militant Shia factions. Tehran has poured millions into Iraq in direct funding for Shia political parties to ensure that the predominant Shia coalition prevailed in the January 2005 elections. Moreover, Iran's close ties with both the Kurds and SCIRI long pre-date U.S. efforts to coalesce the opponents of Saddam.

In southern Iraq, local authorities sympathetic to the Islamic Republic and its strict moral codes have imposed a wide range of restrictions on social and cultural life; there, the perception is that "Iran is running Iraq, frankly speaking," as the spokesman for the Basra-based South Oil Company put it recently.[43] A number of officials in Iraq's interim government, established after the handover of sovereignty by the U.S. occupation administration in June 2004 and disbanded with the elections six months later, complained loudly and frequently about Iran's activities.[44] Hazim Shalan, Iraq's then defense minister, explicitly charged that "Iran interferes in order to kill democracy."[45]

Although U.S. officials regularly remind Baghdad of their own misgivings about Iranian intentions, Washington has effectively acceded to the burgeon-ing ties between the two countries. In contrast to the Bush administration's relentless public pressure vis-à-vis Syria, little or no effort was made to dis-suade the Iraqis from developing a robust and cooperative relationship with Tehran, nor has the United States publicly attempted to exclude Iran from on-going multilateral dialogues related to Iraq. "The Iraqis have relations with their Iranian neighbor and we think that that is a good thing," Secretary of State Rice acknowledged in June 2005. "We have every desire for there to be good relations between Iraq and all of its neighbors, including with Iran."[46]

In the early months after the fall of Saddam, Iran's covert activities were perceived by the United States as generally passive; in other words, "the Ira-nians were in Iraq in strength and were building an intelligence network, but that network was not 'operational'—it was not attempting to do anything other than gather information and strengthen itself."[47] Indeed, Iranian of-ficials and clerics endeavored several times to play a conciliatory role in Iraq, offering to mediate with Sadr. Over time, however, U.S. officials became in-creasingly persuaded that Iran moved from preparing the ground in Iraq to

43. James Hider, "The Violent Undercurrent from Across the Water That Keeps a City on Edge," *Times* (London), July 29, 2005.

44. Doug Struck, "Official Warns of Iranian Infiltration," *Washington Post*, July 26, 2004; Dan Murphy, "Growing Concerns in Baghdad About Iranian Meddling," *Christian Science Monitor*, July 22, 2004.

45. Ibid.

46. Remarks by Secretary Rice made after the International Conference on Iraq in Brus-sels, Belgium, June 22, 2005, www.state.gov/secretary/rm/2005/48471.htm (accessed April 15, 2008).

47. Pollack, *The Persian Puzzle*, 355.

actively supporting and encouraging violence, both against U.S. forces and a variety of Iraqi political actors.

As early as 2004, reports citing U.S. intelligence allege that Iran helped plan for and supply attacks against the coalition forces in Iraq.[48] In addition, in October 2005 the British government publicly blamed Tehran for supplying, either directly or via Lebanese Hezbollah, sophisticated explosive devices to insurgents, who had used them in deadly attacks on UK military forces in southern Iraq.[49] Further reports linked Iran's Revolutionary Guards to training Iraqi insurgents as well.[50] Iranian officials angrily denied the allegations, as did then prime minister Jafari. Over time, the U.S. criticism of Iranian activities in Iraq became more specific and more serious, and in February 2007, President Bush charged what a number of unnamed senior U.S. officials had previously asserted—that the Revolutionary Guards were supplying the munitions that were responsible for the deaths of 170 American soldiers.[51] It was an explosive allegation—attributing American casualties to Tehran for the first time since the 1983 bombings in Beirut—and in the context of heightened tensions over Iran's nuclear activities, expectations of a U.S.-Iranian military confrontation mounted.

Iranian officials rejected the allegations, citing Tehran's assiduous political support for Iraq's elected governments and its extensive involvement in Iraq's economic reconstruction, while deflecting blame for instability in Iraq toward Washington as well as Iraq's Sunni Arab neighbors. "Such allegations are false. They are 100 percent wrong," countered Ali Larijani. "Iran's record of service is clear. You can see the list of our achievements in Iraq, including reconstruction of Iraq. Meanwhile, the same powers, which came there as occupiers and promised to turn it into a beacon of democracy in Iraq, should let us know what they have done."[52]

In December 2006, the United States began to move more aggressively against Iranian agents and activities in Iraq; the seizure of five Iranians based in Irbil described by Washington as members of the Quds Force and by Tehran as diplomats presaged an intensification of the U.S.-Iranian proxy war in Iraq. "We are going after their networks in Iraq," exulted Ambassador Khalilzad

48. Edward T. Pound and Jennifer Jack, "Special Report: The Iran Connection," *U.S. News & World Report*, November 22, 2004.

49. Christopher Adams and Roula Khalaf, "Blair Warns Iran over Iraqi Rebels," *Financial Times* (London), October 6, 2005.

50. Mark Oliver, "Iranian Troops 'Training Iraqi Insurgents,'" *Guardian* (Manchester), October 12, 2005.

51. Sheryl Gay Stolberg and Marc Santora, "Bush Declares Iran's Arms Role in Iraq Is Certain," *New York Times*, February 15, 2007, www.nytimes.com/2007/02/15/world/middleeast/15prexy.html (accessed April 16, 2008).

52. World News Connection, "Larijani: Discusses Nuclear Issue; Improvements in Iraq Due to Iran's Assistance," Islamic Republic of Iran News Network Television, September 13, 2007.

upon the seizure of the five.[53] Tehran responded forcefully in its own time, when in March 2007 Revolutionary Guards seized fifteen British sailors on a routine inspection mission in Iraqi waters in the Persian Gulf. Iran held the sailors for two weeks for allegedly crossing into Iranian territorial waters in a brief crisis that escalated to the Security Council; the final flourish came when Ahmadinejad announced their pardon and release in a public ceremony.

Even as Iranian-American tensions over Iraq escalated, however, new opportunities presented themselves for direct engagement between the two adversaries on Iraqi security. The U.S. envoy in Baghdad had standing authority to talk with his Iranian counterpart, but this channel had never been utilized. Washington gave the cold shoulder to an Iranian public campaign to launch discussions in March 2006, in part because of resistance from Iraqi officials who feared such a meeting would preempt the conclusion of their protracted process of forming a new government. Finally, in May 2007, the two sides agreed to meet in Baghdad for the first of several testy sessions that produced little reason for optimism. Nonetheless, in the ensuing months, U.S. officials began acknowledging positive trends in the supply of Iranian weaponry to Iraqi militants and quietly crediting Iranian intercession for the less confrontational role of Moqtada al Sadr and his militia. Just as the motivations and scope of Iranian malfeasance in Iraq have always been subject to tremendous ambiguity, the same is true for this presumptive new cooperation. Iranian trepidations about new Sunni cooperation with U.S. forces may have also contributed to any change in strategy, particularly in light of the Gulf states' occasional gambits at promoting secular Iraqi leaders such as Iyad Allawi.

The governments of Jordan, Saudi Arabia, and the smaller Gulf sheikhdoms view the growing Iranian-Iraqi amity with wariness and have spoken bluntly about the prospect that the removal of Saddam Hussein has given rise to a "Shia arc" through the heart of the Middle East that will be inherently unstable and antagonistic toward its Sunni neighbors. On the eve of Iraq's first parliamentary elections, King Abdullah of Jordan warned against the emergence of a Shia "crescent . . . that will be very destabilizing for the Gulf countries and for the whole region."[54] Similar suspicions have been regularly voiced by Sunni leaders within Iraq, some of whom have expressed deep misgivings about the ultimate loyalties of particular Shia leaders and the capacity for any post-Saddam government in Iraq to act independently in pursuing the country's national interests. "To us, it seems out of this world that you do this," Saudi Foreign Minister Prince Saud al Faisal told an American

---

53. Louise Roug and Borzou Daragahi, "Iraq Edges Closer to Iran, with or without the U.S.," *Los Angeles Times*, January 16, 2007, www.latimes.com/news/nationworld/world/la-fg-iranians16jan16,1,884473.story?coll=la-headlines-world

54. King Abdullah II, interview by Chris Matthews, *Hardball with Chris Matthews*, MSNBC, December 8, 2004, www.msnbc.msn.com/id/6679774/ (accessed April 16, 2008).

audience in September 2005. "We fought a war together to keep Iran from occupying Iraq after Iraq was driven out of Kuwait. Now we are handing the whole country over to Iran without reason."[55]

While Iran's newfound regional sway came courtesy of an independent, albeit interrelated, set of internal developments in Iraq, Lebanon, and among the Palestinians, it was interpreted by both the United States and many of Iran's neighbors as the product of a deliberate Iranian policy of renewed regional subversion, rather than the shrewd exploitation of opportunities. Defeating "Iran's bid for regional hegemony" emerged as a new U.S. talking point. "Everywhere you turn, it is the policy of Iran to foment instability and chaos, no matter the strategic value or cost in the blood of innocents," Secretary of Defense Robert Gates said in December 2007.[56]

But Washington sought to transform this strategic deficit into an advantage through alliance-building. The Bush administration viewed the summer 2006 war in Lebanon as a strategic shift of momentous proportions in the regional climate. At the time, Rice was widely lambasted for her tin-ear assertion that the war represented "the birth pangs of a new Middle East,"[57] but in the ensuing months the United States endeavored to capitalize on trepidations among the leading Sunni Arab states about the rising tide of Iranian influence in order to leverage their support for a revived Arab-Israeli peace process. A number of pundits suggested that Arab leaders' interest in blunting Tehran's efforts within the Levant would generate unprecedented willingness within Gulf capitals to provide the financial support and diplomatic traction necessary to generate new progress toward an Israeli-Palestinian settlement. To date, a variety of factors—including the weakness of the Israeli government, the escalation of intra-Palestinian violence, and the general disinclination of the Gulf Cooperation Council (GCC) states to extend themselves on behalf of the Palestinians—has undercut any momentum along these lines.

How Iran's assertion of power in Iraq will play out on a broader Middle East stage is an issue of increasing attention and concern. Regional fears of a revived and coordinated Shia arc of influence are to some extent self-serving. Casting blame toward Iran for the chaos in Iraq effectively deflects any responsibility from Iraq's Sunni neighbors, most of whom have done less than they might be expected to do to advance stability, democracy, and prosperity in Iraq and some of whom—particularly Saudi

---

55. Prince Saud Al Faisal, remarks at the Council on Foreign Relations discussion on "The Fight Against Extremism and the Search for Peace," New York, September 20, 2005, www. cfr.org/publication/8908/fight_against_extremism_and_the_search_for_peace_rush_ transcript_federal_news_service_inc.html (accessed April 16, 2008).

56. Ann Scott Tyson, "Iran Aims 'To Foment Instability,' Gates Says," *Washington Post*, December 9, 2007.

57. Secretary of State Condoleezza Rice, Special Briefing on Travel to the Middle East and Europe, July 21, 2006, www.state.gov/secretary/rm/2006/69331.htm (accessed April 16, 2008).

Arabia—bear their own share of responsibility for the violence in Iraq because of their citizens' involvement in the insurgency.[58] Moreover, the cultural and political revival of the Shia world need not represent an inherent threat to its Sunni neighbors. Although the Islamic Republic poses very real challenges to the United States and other key states in the region, nationalist imperatives will continue to dominate its decision making. In addition, any Shia resurgence will fuel the ongoing theological and policy-oriented debates about the role of religion in politics.[59]

Further, the most important variable in the stability of states with significant Shia minorities—such as Bahrain, Saudi Arabia, Kuwait, and Pakistan—will be the overall tenor of these states' domestic politics, particularly on minority rights issues. Since the early years of the Iranian revolution, the Gulf states have undergone meaningful internal evolution and their leaderships have made copious efforts to address the concerns of historically marginalized communities or, at minimum, to co-opt their Shia populations. The Saudi "national dialogue," Bahrain's embrace of limited democracy, and the flourishing of a dysfunctional Kuwaiti parliament all signify the reasonably successful incorporation of the Gulf Shia into their respective national polities. As a result, the relative quiescence of the region's minority Shia populations is unlikely to be dramatically altered by virtue of either a demonstration effect or even direct patronage from Shia powerhouses such as Iran or Iraq. As regional expert Moshe Maoz argues, the threat posed by the rise of Shiism in the region "is largely a myth that masks important, but malleable state interests. By rejecting this myth, the United States can see the Shia in the Middle East for what they are: varied communities with as much dividing them as uniting them, potential partners in some places, aspiring adversaries in others."[60]

Nonetheless, the perception of—and the potential reaction to—a "Shia crescent" arguably represents the true threat to regional peace and stability. A realignment of the current uneasy balance of power along sectarian lines may well be triggered not by the political dominance of Iraqi Shia, but by the effects of misguided policies by some Sunni-dominated governments intended to counter some mythical Shia threat. Based on the dynamics unleashed after the birth of the Islamic Republic, it is entirely conceivable that other critical regional actors, such as Pakistan and Saudi Arabia, may respond to the new alignment of political power in the broader Middle

58. Susan Glasser, "'Martyrs' in Iraq Mostly Saudis," *Washington Post*, May 15, 2005.

59. Vali Nasr, *The Shia Revival: How Conflicts within Islam Will Shape the Future* (New York: W.W. Norton, 2006).

60. Moshe Maoz, *The "Shi'i Crescent": Myth and Reality* (Brookings Institution, Saban Center for Middle East Policy Analysis Paper no. 15, November 2007), www.brookings. edu/~/media/Files/rc/papers/2007/11_middle_east_maoz/11_middle_east_maoz. pdf (accessed April 16, 2008).

East by propagating dogmatic theological philosophies and institutions or by reflexively seeking to undermine post-Saddam Iraq simply because of its leadership's Shia composition. In an already fertile environment for Sunni radicalism, significant state support would be incendiary.

The combination of the shifts in the regional balance of power and Ahmadinejad's extremism provided a powerful incentive for the Arab states of the Persian Gulf to strengthen their security relationship with Washington. However, despite their significant misgivings about Iran and their intensifying defense relationships with Washington, the Arab states of the Persian Gulf have made clear that they will not form the bulwark of an anti-Iranian coalition. The Saudis have hosted Ahmadinejad several times, including—for the first time ever—for the Iranian president's performance of the hajj in December 2007. Riyadh also undoubtedly sanctioned another unprecedented act of regional comity, Ahmadinejad's participation in the annual summit of the leaders of the GCC in December 2007, where he proposed a regional security pact and new economic cooperation between Iran and its historic adversaries.

For their part, Iran's leaders have demonstrated some awareness of the need to maintain a constructive relationship with Riyadh and the Gulf states. Tehran has repeatedly dispatched envoys to Riyadh over the past several years to assuage concerns over Ahmadinejad's rhetoric and Iran's escalating tensions with the West. For example, former foreign minister Velayati, the supreme leader's personal adviser on foreign affairs, was sent to do damage control after Ahmadinejad's outrageous performance at the December 2005 summit of the Organization of the Islamic Conference (OIC). As Ali Larijani commented, "There are forces at play both inside Saudi Arabia and in the region who do not want Iran and Saudi to have good relations. Iran and Saudi are two mighty Muslim nations. There is high-level dialogue. Mistakes are possible in any country. These mistakes should be resolved in the political process and through dialogue. I think the issue is being [unnecessarily] intensified and this is exacerbating the situation. We do have our disagreements in certain areas, but overall the relations between Iran and Saudi are very dignified with excellent underpinning."[61] Larijani also traveled to Cairo in December 2007 to reinvigorate long-stalled discussions with the Egyptian government about upgrading their relationship to full diplomatic ties.

---

61. "Larijani Discusses Nuclear Issue; Improvements in Iraq Due to Iran's Assistance," Islamic Republic of Iran News Network Television, September 13, 2007, World News Connection.

Bid for "Extraregional" Influence

Of central concern to the Middle East and the broader Islamic world is Iran's nuclear program. Iran's efforts to obtain a nuclear weapons option—consistently denied by the Islamic regime but manifestly evident from its activities and long-standing patterns of deception—evoke a complex set of concerns for the Muslim world. First and foremost, these programs pose a direct and immediate threat given Iran's history of regional ambitions and antagonism; a nuclear-armed Iran would wield decisive leverage and have the capacity to wholly destabilize the Persian Gulf. It is possible—though by no means certain—that a nuclear weapons capability would embolden the more aggressive tendencies of Iran's foreign policy, loosening constraints that might currently check more radical initiatives and undercutting trends toward a more pragmatic pursuit of its national interests.

However any nuclear breakthrough might shape Iran's own foreign policy decision making, it certainly would have a negative impact on the strategic perceptions of its neighbors and raise the prestige value of this and other weapons of mass destruction (WMD) in the broader Middle East. Equally problematic would be the inevitable quest for enhanced influence and efforts to "contain" an intensified Iranian threat by other aspiring regional hegemons, such as Saudi Arabia. Renewed initiatives by Iran's neighbors to project their own power beyond their borders would likely exacerbate already heightened tensions in the region, and would have ripple effects far beyond the immediate environs of the Islamic Republic. Finally, Iran's WMD activities establish a secondary set of security concerns by intensifying the reliance of the Persian Gulf states on the U.S. security umbrella and by exacerbating the potential for conflict between Tehran and Washington—conflict that could present serious internal frictions for other Muslim states with populations predisposed to sympathize with a perceived "Islamic bomb."

Iran's nuclear aspirations long predate the Islamic Revolution and in fact are grounded in what was once its vital alliance with the United States. In the mid-1960s, with the full support of Washington, Iran's monarchy began developing its nuclear capabilities, building research centers and launching efforts to train Iranians in the technology at home and abroad. In conjunction with this effort, Tehran signed the Nuclear Nonproliferation Treaty (NPT) in 1968 and the Iranian parliament ratified it two years later. The monarchy awarded a contract to build two nuclear power plants to a German company in 1974, and construction began near the port city of Bushehr over the following two years. Another deal for an additional two 900MW nuclear reactors was eventually signed with a French company in 1977, and the Shah envisioned as many as twenty-three reactors to be built by U.S., French, and German companies. While these plans were justified on the basis of the power generation needs of a rapidly expanding economy, it is also clear that the monarchy intended to use its peaceful nuclear program as camouflage and a launching pad for an ongoing weapons research effort.[62]

In the initial aftermath of the revolution, the clerical regime abrogated Iran's existing contracts for nuclear plants and jettisoned plans for a national nuclear infrastructure as religiously proscribed and wasteful. That view was steadily reversed, however, during the course of the eight-year war with Iraq, whose overwhelming missile superiority and use of chemical weapons against Iranian forces persuaded the leadership in Tehran to set about reconstituting its own WMD efforts. The unfinished Bushehr plant, which had been partially damaged by repeated Iraqi attacks, resurfaced as the focus of Iran's civilian nuclear program (and the focus of U.S. efforts to preclude Iranian WMD acquisition). After protracted negotiations with a range of European companies failed, in part because of U.S. pressure, Tehran approached China and the Soviet Union, signing a preliminary deal with Moscow in 1990. Another five years passed—marked by concerted and wide-ranging efforts by the Iranians to procure necessary components for Bushehr and its other nuclear activities through a variety of third countries—before a final contract was ultimately signed.

The light water reactor at Bushehr routinely emerged as a point of tension in U.S.-Russian relations during the Clinton administration and early years of the Bush administration. However, that project itself is not generally considered to constitute a weapons threat except insofar as it provides cover for a wider range of research, training, and procurement activities. It is these patterns of Iranian behavior that raised considerable alarm in Washington for more than a decade. Together with the subsequent revelations about Iran's clandestine efforts to build an indigenous enrichment capability, the scope of Iran's nuclear program, combined with U.S. pressure, has persuaded most other governments—with the notable exceptions of Russia, China, Pakistan, and North Korea—to abstain from nuclear cooperation with Iran.

As with its nuclear program, Iran is a signatory to both major international agreements concerning biological and chemical weapons—the Biological and Toxin Weapons Convention (BWC, ratified in 1973) and the Chemical Weapons Convention (CWC, ratified in 1997). Notwithstanding these treaty obligations and Tehran's denials, the United States alleges that Iran began reconstituting its weapons programs in both arenas during the 1980s. Verifiable public evidence is minimal, but most experts appear to agree that Iran maintains a small stockpile of biological agents and an increasingly sophisticated chemical program.

Iran's missile programs also expanded dramatically during the 1980s, largely in response to the persistent effectiveness demonstrated by Iraq's use

---

62. Anthony H. Cordesman, *Iran & Iraq: The Threat from the Northern Gulf* (Boulder, CO: Westview Press, 1994), 103–04.

of these weapons in striking Iranian forces and population centers. Tehran's initial efforts focused on procurement, with acquisitions of Scud-C and Scud-B missiles from Libya, North Korea, Russia, and China. Subsequently, Iran began investing in its indigenous production capabilities and has since developed an infrastructure to construct short- and medium-range missiles. After several years of abortive tests, Iran successfully fired the Shehab-3—which, with its 1,300-km range is capable of reaching Israel—in 2000, and it has since entered limited production and been officially placed into active service. Concerns also focus on Iranian efforts to develop longer-range or even intercontinental ballistic missiles (ICBMs) known as the Shehab-4 and -5, but evidence to date suggests Iran is unlikely to achieve the technical capability to launch an ICBM.

Given its history and its turbulent neighborhood, Iran's WMD ambitions do not reflect a wholly irrational set of strategic calculations by its leadership. While the low-intensity threats emanating from Central Asia and Afghanistan represent considerable security interests for Tehran, these issues remain distinctly secondary in the array of Iran's strategic priorities, which historically have been oriented westward. The Iranian leadership remains preoccupied with countering the threat from Iraq, realizing its rightful place as a (or even "the") dominant power in the Gulf, and fending off potential intervention by the United States. For these purposes, many Iranians perceive that a nuclear capability would present a potent instrument of defense and deterrence.

Arguments for enhancing Iran's nuclear capabilities are necessarily pursued in private more often than public forums, particularly since Ahmadinejad's embrace of the issue has limited the options for public discussion within Iran. Nonetheless, the rationales behind Iran's pursuit of a nuclear option can be elucidated from the rich literature on security issues that is present in the Iranian press and academic journals. In addition to the prodigious sense of insecurity inculcated by the Iraqi invasion and the experience of the war itself, there appears to be widespread consensus surrounding two other important consequences of WMD—prestige and leverage. The former reflects the deeply held national pride that is a distinctly Iranian characteristic. From this perspective, it is simply inconceivable to Iranians across the political spectrum that neighboring Pakistan, a country considered to be greatly inferior in terms of its economy, society, and political maturity, should have more advanced military technology. The second factor that pervades Iranian consideration of its nuclear options—leverage—exposes further the fundamental strategic deficiencies of its continuing estrangement from the United States. For many in Tehran, maintaining some sort of viable nuclear program offers the single most valuable enhancement of the country's bargaining position with Washington.

This perspective has been strengthened inadvertently and unfortunately by the campaign to unseat Saddam Hussein in Iraq and the tacit U.S. acquiescence of North Korea's nuclear capability. An Israeli analyst has described Iran's nuclear program as its "security bond" against regime change. "They look at the international arena and see how the United States brought down Saddam's regime because he didn't have nuclear weapons and they see how the Americans are using kid gloves against North Korea, which has violated all agreements it has signed, because it has nuclear weapons. . . . Iran wants international immunity."[63]

The elimination of Saddam Hussein has unequivocally mitigated one of Iran's most serious security concerns. Yet regime change in Iraq has left Tehran with potential chaos along its vulnerable western border, and an ever more proximate American capability to project power in the region. In fact, together with provocative U.S. rhetoric on the issue of regime change, rogue states, and preemptive action, recent changes in the regional balance of power have only enhanced the potential deterrent value of a "strategic weapon" to Iran's leadership. Moreover, the experience of the war with Iraq remains imprinted in the memories of Iran's leadership—the isolation that hampered its early defense, the relative indifference with which the international community greeted Iraq's use of chemical weapons against Iranian troops, and the profound technological inferiority that left Iran so vulnerable to the initial Iraqi incursion and, later, to Iraqi missiles.[64]

Unlike Iran's other provocative policies, which have generated intrafactional debate and thereby played into the internal power struggle, the nuclear temptation appears to generate broad consensus across the Iranian political spectrum. Opponents of crossing the nuclear threshold remain vocal and influential; still, it is clear that nuclear potential resonates with a collective set of interests that do not divide neatly between Iran's political factions. The prestige factor and the apparent deterrent that a nuclear capability represents offer powerful incentives for both reformers and conservatives. There are greater divisions over the utility of confrontation with the international community than a nuclear capability. While moderates emphasize the benefits of Iran's regional détente and its commercial relations with Europe and Asia, hard-liners are not deterred by a prospect of international sanctions and isolation and would welcome a crisis as a means of rekindling Iran's waning revolutionary fires and deflecting attention from the domestic deficiencies of Islamic rule.

---

63. Arieh O'Sullivan, "Target: The Jewish State," *Jerusalem Post*, November 25, 2004.

64. Fred Halliday, "The Iranian Revolution and International Politics," in *Iran at the Crossroads*, eds. John L. Esposito and R.K. Ramazani (New York: Palgrave, 2001), 182. It is worth noting that Iraq's prodigious Scud capabilities enabled it to inflict considerable damage on Iranian civilians far beyond the war front, killing an estimated 2,226 and wounding another 10,705.

Over the past several years, Iran's construction of extensive uranium enrichment facilities became evident through the work of U.S. intelligence and follow-up inquiries by the International Atomic Energy Agency (IAEA). Hitherto undeclared, the disclosures of the research facilities in Natanz and Tehran together with a heavy water production plant in Arak, a uranium conversion plant in Isfahan, and the acknowledgment of significant imports of uranium from China transformed the urgency of intelligence estimates surrounding Iran's nuclear capabilities and the time remaining before it may reach a nuclear threshold. These discoveries, and more recent disclosures, have also given rise to new doubts about the credibility of Iranian commitment to abide by the terms of the NPT, as it appears to be pursuing multiple routes to acquire fissile material.

The alarming nature of the disclosures helped to generate rare multilateral consensus to admonish Iran, as did the coincidental emergence of new irritants in Iran's previously smooth relations with Canada and Argentina—whose governments then served on the IAEA Board of Governors. In October 2003, the international pressure produced a small and ultimately ephemeral compromise when Iran agreed to disclose its nuclear activities; sign the Additional Protocol, which authorized unannounced intensive inspections of all its nuclear sites; and suspend its uranium enrichment activities.

However, frictions in Iran's interaction with the IAEA and new revelations about the true extent of Iranian nuclear activities paved the way for further confrontations. Iran grudgingly lived up to some of its agreements, suspending uranium enrichment and signing the Additional Protocol in December 2003, albeit without parliamentary ratification. In November 2004, the Iranian government once again struck a deal with its primary European interlocutors (Great Britain, France, and Germany, the so-called EU-3) that extended and expanded its self-declared "temporary" suspension of all enrichment and reprocessing related activities while negotiations toward a long-term arrangement that provided "objective guarantees that Iran's nuclear program is exclusively for peaceful purposes." In exchange, the EU-3 promised to launch discussions on "political and security issues" as well as "technology and cooperation," and pledged active support for Iran's bid to begin accession talks with the World Trade Organization (WTO).[65] In support of the European effort, Washington announced in March 2005 that it would drop its long-standing objection to Iran's application to enter discussions with the WTO and followed through on that pledge three months later.

---

65. "Communication Dated 26 November 2004 Received from the Permanent Representatives of France, Germany, the Islamic Republic of Iran and the United Kingdom Concerning the Agreement Signed in Paris on 15 November 2004," IAEA Information Circular INFCIRC/637, November 26, 2004, www.iaea.org/Publications/Documents/Infcircs/2004/infcirc637.pdf (accessed April 16, 2008).

Nonetheless, Iran repeatedly indulged in brinkmanship while dealing with the Europeans and the IAEA, threatening to end the temporary suspension and abrogate the Paris Accord. Tehran finally made good on its threats in August 2005 when the government resumed activities at its uranium conversion facility located in Isfahan. Although the decision to end its suspension of enrichment and reprocessing-related activities under the Paris Accord appears to have commanded support from across the political spectrum—the outgoing Khatami administration notified the IAEA of the decision on August 1—much attention focused on the role of Iran's new president, who was inaugurated on August 6, two days before uranium conversion actually resumed in Isfahan. However the decision may have been made, this step—together with the replacement of most of Iran's nuclear negotiating team and Ahmadinejad's provocative rhetoric and policies—cemented the perception of renewed intransigence in Tehran. In September 2005, the IAEA found Iran in noncompliance with its NPT obligations, moving the issue on a path to the UN Security Council.

Effectively brushing off the mounting involvement of the Security Council, Tehran pushed forward aggressively with its nuclear activities, resuming uranium enrichment in February 2006 and declaring its nuclear activities to be "irreversible." The program moved forward with remarkable alacrity, with each technical milestone celebrated by Iran's leadership in splashy and highly politicized fashion. By mid-2008, Iran had three thousand operating centrifuges, with plans to install another six thousand by year's end. Ironically, even as Ahmadinejad's rhetoric helped coalesce an unprecedented degree of international consensus on forestalling Iran's nuclear program, Tehran's very obstinacy and the failure of successive proposals by the Europeans, Russians, and other international actors generated new impetus for more robust U.S. diplomacy. In May 2006, the Bush administration reversed three years of rejecting any contact with Tehran, as well as its long-standing opposition to even civil nuclear activities in Iran. In concert with European allies as well as Russia and China, it offered to join negotiations with Tehran and put forward a package of incentives on the condition that Iran resume its suspension of its enrichment and reprocessing activities.

The overture was intended to offer Iran a strategic choice between moderation or isolation, and enhance American leverage beyond the unappealing alternatives of military force and an arduous, unsatisfying route at the United Nations. Secretary Rice made clear that the offer was not intended to initiate a grand bargain, nor was it a path toward normalization.[66] For its part, the Iranian leadership remained firm on its

---

66. Secretary of State Condoleezza Rice, interview by Chris Wallace, *Fox News Sunday*, Fox, June 4, 2006, www.state.gov/secretary/rm/2006/67502.htm (accessed April 16, 2008); in-

opposition to any further suspension of enrichment and calculated that it could withstand whatever economic pressure the international community might muster. In December 2006, and again in February 2007 and March 2008, the Security Council passed successive sanctions resolutions that banned outside assistance to Iran's enrichment and reprocessing activities and imposed a selective asset freeze and other restrictions on individuals and organizations associated with the nuclear program.

For a brief moment, the Bush administration argued that it had gained some traction vis-à-vis Iran. "There was a period of time over the autumn when a lot of people in the press and academic experts, even some people in government, were saying the Iranians seem to be doing very well," Undersecretary of State Nicholas Burns, the Bush administration's point person on Iran, said in February 2007. "And yet what happened over the last six or seven weeks?. . . All of a sudden in the middle of February the Iranians are not doing so well, the Iranians are now questioning their own strategy, and I think that is what is interesting and hopeful about this diplomatic process."[67]

Fast forward a year, and what Burns and others saw as a turning point seems to have been a mirage. In a stunning turn of events, Washington released an unclassified summary of a National Intelligence Estimate (NIE) on Iran's nuclear program that at first blush appeared to vindicate Tehran. The report concluded that, "In fall 2003, Tehran halted its nuclear weapons program," but its corollary assessment that Iran is "at minimum" keeping its nuclear options open received relatively short shrift in the breathless press coverage of the report.[68] Ahmadinejad gloated that the report signified "a clear surrender" by Washington,[69] and the modest progress that Washington had made toward achieving consensus on a third Security Council resolution over six months of fruitless international negotiations quickly receded. Several days after the report's release, Moscow dispatched a long-delayed shipment of fuel for the Bushehr nuclear power plant—a tacit acknowledgment that the international community was beginning to shrug off some of the voluntary constraints on engagement with Iran's nuclear program.

At home, the report totally transformed the debate on dealing with Iran's nuclear ambitions. As Senator Joseph Biden warned, "War with

terview by Wolf Blitzer, *CNN's Late Edition*, CNN, June 4, 2006, www.state.gov/secretary/rm/2006/67506.htm (accessed April 16, 2008).

67. R. Nicholas Burns, undersecretary of state for political affairs, "A Conversation on Iran and U.S. National Security," remarks to the Brookings Institution, February 14, 2007, www.state.gov/p/us/rm/2007/80562.htm (accessed April 16, 2008).

68. National Intelligence Council, National Intelligence Estimate, "Iran: Nuclear Intentions and Capabilities," November 2007, www.dni.gov/press_releases/20071203_release.pdf (accessed April 16, 2008).

69. President Mahmoud Ahmadinejad, interview on Islamic Republic of Iran Broadcasting Network One, December 16, 2007, translated by BBC Monitoring.

Iran is not just a bad option. It would be a disaster. That's why I want to be very clear: if the President takes us to war with Iran without Congressional approval, I will call for his impeachment. I do not say this lightly or to be provocative. I am dead serious. I have chaired the Senate Judiciary Committee. I still teach constitutional law. I've consulted with some of our leading constitutional scholars. The Constitution is clear. And so am I."[70]

Despite the easing of international trepidations over the prospect of a U.S.-Iranian military conflict as a result of the NIE, there appears to be little prospect of a quick or easy resolution of this dispute. The Bush administration has given little indication that it is prepared to countenance the continuation of Iran's enrichment and reprocessing activities—and yet neither its punitive measures nor the package of incentives promised as part of the negotiations proposal have had a discernible positive impact with respect to Iran's determination to expand its nuclear infrastructure. Although some Democratic presidential candidates have endorsed negotiations without preconditions, it is difficult to imagine any administration in Washington that will readily abandon this redline without significant confidence-building gestures from the Iranian side.

Conversely, the Iranian government has repeatedly—and almost universally—insisted that Tehran will never cede its right under the NPT to enrich uranium or otherwise cede access to nuclear technology and activities. The hard-liners associated with Ahmadinejad have long disparaged both the process and the outcome of Iran's dealings with the IAEA and its negotiations with the EU-3. Influential conservative politician Ali Larijani, who later served as nuclear negotiator but resigned over tensions with Ahmadinejad, blasted the November 2004 Paris Accord as a case in which Iran "gave a fine pearl, and received candy" in return.[71] And while the fallout from the Security Council action has revived the debate within Tehran on the handling of the nuclear issue, the divisions within Iran's political elite do not appear to extend beyond the *style* of the government's approach to the actual *substance* of the program.[72] Meanwhile, having couched Iran's nuclear stance in staunchly nationalist terms, Iran's

---

70. Senator Joe Biden, speech given at the Iowa City Public Library, December 3, 2007, www. cfr.org/publication/14976/joe_bidens_speech_on_iran.html (accessed April 16, 2008).

71. Guy Dinmore and Gareth Smyth, "Iran Nuclear Deal 'a Fine Pearl in Return for Candy'," *Financial Times* (London), November 17, 2004.

72. This debate began in the days after Ahmadinejad's address to the UN General Assembly, when editorials in the Iranian press criticized the speech and the failure of Iran's negotiators to prevent the noncompliance finding by the IAEA. In his September 30 sermon at Tehran's Friday prayers, former president Rafsanjani advised Ahmadinejad's new administration that "You need diplomacy and not slogans." See Karl Vick, "Iran Moves to Curb Hard-liners," *Washington Post*, October 8, 2005. Further critiques were made episodically by Ruhani as well as Larijani's after Larijani's resignation as nuclear negotiator.

flexibility on this issue—particularly for a government that has staked its claim to legitimacy on populist appeals—has become more limited than ever. The May 2007 arrest and subsequent conviction of Hossein Moussavian, a senior member of the nuclear negotiating team during the Khatami era, on espionage charges sent a chilling signal that public criticism of the regime's nuclear ambitions—even from well-connected insiders—would not be permitted.

Iran's neighbors generally maintain a convenient quiet with respect to Iran's nuclear program, refraining from public statements to avoid exacerbating historic tensions with Tehran. Saudi Defense Minister Prince Sultan bin Abdul Aziz has dismissed a possible Iranian nuclear attack on Arab Gulf countries, calling Iran "a friendly state." Commenting on Iran's controversial nuclear program and the perception of it by GCC states, Prince Sultan pointedly noted that he does not believe Iran "will think one day of jeopardizing the security of the peoples of the GCC states."[73] Dubai-based analyst Riad Kahwaji notes that irrespective of recent discussion about a regional missile defense system, none of the GCC states has engaged in civil defense planning in preparation for a potential Iranian strike, and characterizes the predominant regional perception—apart from Saudi Arabia—of Iran's WMD capabilities and intentions as "indifferent."[74]

Privately, however, U.S. and European officials suggest that the Gulf states in particular harbor significant concerns about Iran's nuclear ambitions, in part because it increases their own dependence on the U.S. security umbrella.[75] For the Gulf, Iran's nuclear ambitions "intensify foreign military presence in the region and force regional states into an arms race that could adversely affect regional stability, deepen mistrust, and obstruct national development plans."[76] More pointedly, the Gulf states are profoundly averse to developments that would destabilize the regional balance of power and further strengthen Iran's already intensifying sway in the post-Saddam Hussein security landscape, and they have sharpened their discourse accordingly. At their December 2006 annual summit, the GCC leaders went beyond their standard call for a regionwide ban on nuclear weapons—a subtle dig at Israel that renders the call effectively futile—and explicitly addressed the Iranian nuclear dispute, emphasizing the need for a peaceful resolution, urging Iran to cooperate with the IAEA, and pledging to launch

73. "Saudi Prince Calls Iran a 'Friendly State,'" *Washington Times*, January 10, 2005.
74. Riad Kahwaji, "U.S.-Arab Cooperation in the Gulf," *Middle East Policy* 11, no. 3 (Fall 2004): 59.
75. Roula Khalaf, "Iranian Nuclear Ambitions Worry Gulf Arab States," *Financial Times* (London), December 18, 2004.
76. Abdulaziz Sager, "For Saudi Arabia and Iran, Searching for Security Is a Priority," *Daily Star* (Beirut), June 13, 2005.

a GCC civil nuclear program.[77] For the Islamic world further afield, the Iranian nuclear issue tends to be viewed through the prism of other interests vis-à-vis both Tehran and Washington.

The primary uncertainty for the United States as well as for the Muslim world concerns how Iran's leadership might behave if the country were to cross the nuclear threshold. By transforming the regional balance of power, nuclear weapons "could therefore alter the decision calculus of Iran's clerical leadership" and empower a reinvigorated radicalism unconstrained by resources or capabilities.[78] Iranian leaders have publicly rejected any intention to develop or utilize WMD as un-Islamic, and one of Iran's most senior clerics has described this position as an irreversible function of "eternal law."[79] However, Iran's history of deception in the development of its nuclear facilities appropriately raises skepticism about this stance, as does its rhetoric toward Israel and its episodic invocation of the utility of nuclear weapons, such as a sermon given by Rafsanjani in 2001:

> If one day, the Islamic world is also equipped with weapons like those that Israel possesses now, then the imperialists' strategy will reach a standstill because the use of even one nuclear bomb inside Israel will destroy everything. However, it will only harm the Islamic world. It is not irrational to contemplate such an eventuality. Of course, you can see that the Americans have kept their eyes peeled and they are carefully looking for even the slightest hint that technological advances are being made by an independent Islamic country. If an independent Islamic country is thinking about acquiring other kinds of weaponry, then they will do their utmost to prevent it from acquiring them.[80]

Even where it may be deliberately hyperbolic or hypothetical, such rhetoric inevitably shapes the strategic context, particularly where it is consistent with a broader adversarial relationship.

Concerns that a nuclear-armed Iran would be tempted to lend its capabilities to terrorist organizations—particularly those such as Hezbollah and Palestinian Islamic Jihad with which it has a long-standing relationship—are justified but probably overblown. Nonetheless, as regional expert Kenneth Pollack puts it, "This regime has demonstrated that it is ag-

---

77. "Closing Statement of the Twenty-Seventh Session of the Supreme Council of the Cooperation Council for the Arab States of the Gulf (GCC)," Riyadh, December 9–10, 2006, http://library.gcc-sg.org/English/Books/sessions/cs027.html (accessed April 16, 2008).

78. Michael Eisenstadt, *Iranian Military Power Capabilities and Intentions* (Washington, DC: Washington Institute for Near East Policy, 1996), 25.

79. Robert Collier, "Nuclear Weapons Unholy, Iran Says," *San Francisco Chronicle*, October 31, 2003.

80. Akbar Hashemi Rafsanjani Friday prayer sermon, delivered in Tehran on December 14, 2001, broadcast on the Voice of the Islamic Republic of Iran, translated by BBC Monitoring.

gressive, anti-status quo, anti-American, and willing to employ a host of reprehensible methods (such as terrorism) to try to accomplish its goals. While it may be possible to live with such a regime after it has acquired nuclear weapons, most non-Iranians would prefer not to have to try to do so, if it could be avoided."[81]

The question of how the prospect of Iran's acquisition of nuclear weapons might be avoided also has particular salience for the Islamic world. The region and other critical Muslim actors have generally tried to maintain their distance where possible and achieve some general balance between the prerequisites of good global citizenship and maintaining cooperative relations with both Washington and Tehran. Ultimately, religious ties have not shielded Iran from international opprobrium. A number of predominantly Muslim states as well as Iran's traditional allies among the Non-Aligned Movement voted to refer Tehran's case to the UN Security Council in 2005. Meanwhile, the only Muslim country on the 2007 Security Council, Qatar, tried to finesse the contending camps with an abstention on the first resolution and efforts to shape the second—a position that undoubtedly irritated both capitals.

The alternative means of contending with the Iranian nuclear program also provoke significant concerns from the Muslim world. Iran's neighbors with robust relations with Washington are already finding it difficult to finesse the precipitous divide between two governments. Were the international community to coalesce around a vigorous sanctions regime along the lines of the multilateral embargo on Libya in response to the Lockerbie bombing, Iran's neighbors would face significant implications for their own economies as well as retributive acts by Tehran. A preemptive U.S. or Israeli strike on Iranian nuclear facilities would inevitably generate significant popular discontent across the Islamic world. In January 2005, Malaysian Defense Minister Najib Razak suggested that "hard and irrefutable evidence" would be necessary to demonstrate to the world that Iran presented a threat and added that any military action against Iran would be "of great concern" to the Islamic world.[82]

Rial Diplomacy: Iran's Economic Influence

One of Ayatollah Khomeini's many infamous aphorisms was his declaration that the revolution was not about the price of melons. While the economy may not have been a central issue for the icon of the Islamic Republic, in fact it constitutes a central component of Iran's influence. With approximately 10 percent of the world's proven oil reserves, and 15 percent of the world's natural gas reserves, Iran plays a major role in the world economy, and in

---

81. Pollack, *The Persian Puzzle*, 378.
82. "Malaysia Warns US Against Attacking Iran," Agence France-Presse, January 23, 2005.

turn finds its domestic options and imperatives inextricably linked to the world beyond its borders.

As Khomeini's dismissive perspective evidences, the Islamic Republic has struggled to develop an effective approach to its own economy. As will be explored further in the following section, Iran's postrevolutionary leadership was sharply divided on basic issues of economic philosophy and policy. At the root of this division was a fundamental disagreement over Islam's sanction of and compatibility with capitalism. The conservative clergy, in tandem with *bazaaris*, their allies in Iran's traditional marketplace, argued that Islam in fact sanctified private property and private enterprise. However, they found themselves fending off the socialist-inspired impulses of the radical faction of the revolutionary coalition, who placed primacy on the role of the state in promoting social justice. The contention between these two factions dominated much of the early decision making in the postrevolutionary period; one of the fiercest battles during this time was fought over the question of nationalizing foreign trade. The traditionalist-conservative faction ultimately prevailed in this particular debate, but the questions of how and how much Iran's economy ought to be integrated into the international arena remained hotly disputed. The flawed reconstruction and adjustment program implemented in the 1990s by then-president Hashemi Rafsanjani only raised further sensitivities in this regard by generating a considerable debt burden for Iran in a very short period. Even today, the issue of foreign investment continues to provoke controversy within Iran's polarized political classes.[83]

This is, of course, one of the many ironies associated with the Islamic Republic because its economy was and remains inextricably interlinked with the international energy industry. Although Iranian leaders intensely debated the revolutionary state's orientation to the world, there was never any consideration of withdrawing from the global oil markets; Khomeini himself called the industry "the lifeblood of the nation" and the prime minister of Iran's provisional government warned that the revolution would fail without the resumption of oil exports.[84] And while Iranian officials have occasionally indulged in rhetorical brandishing of the oil card, the regime's reliance on oil revenues and hawkish position in the Organization of Petroleum Exporting Countries (OPEC) mean any threat to pull its exports from the market has limited credibility. As a result, although the Islamic Republic prohibited any international involvement in the extraction of its oil and gas resources until 1990, every aspect of Iran's economy—and

---

83. The Foreign Investment Promotion and Protection Act (FIPPA) was ratified in May 2002 by the Expediency Council after protracted debate between the reformist parliament and the Council of Guardians. FIPPA replaced the outdated 1956 Law on the Attraction and Promotion of Foreign Investment.

84. Ramazani, *Revolutionary Iran*, 206–07.

Figure 1. Iran's Trade with the Muslim World (1979–2005) *as a percentage of total trade*

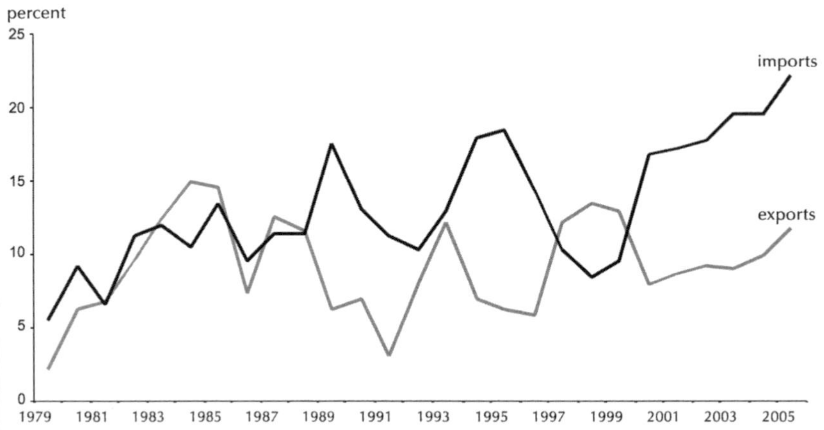

its society—is shaped in some way by the forces of worldwide supply and demand for energy resources.

Although the Iranian government's rhetoric has placed a primacy on its economic relationships with the Muslim world, the impact this rhetoric—either on the flows of Iranian trade and investment or on the nature of the overall Iranian relationship with the Islamic world—is not apparent. Iran's trade with the Islamic world has expanded since the revolution and generally has risen as a proportion of Iran's total trade, but remains modest. As figure 1 suggests, in recent years as Iran's economy has expanded—in concert with oil prices—so has its economic engagement with the Muslim world.[85]

Not surprisingly, given its history of antagonism and the generalized vectors for most regional capital flows, only a small proportion of the foreign direct investment that Iran has managed to attract comes from the Muslim world. Most of the foreign capital for Iran's energy sector has come from the major international companies based in Europe and Asia, although Iran's slow progress in developing its gas resources and difficulty in securing major new markets has opened up modest opportunities for exports via pipeline within the region. Historically, the major investors in Iran's nonoil sector have included Canada and Europe (Italy, Luxembourg, and France).[86] Although more recent statistics are not available, anecdotal

---

85. Statistical, Economic and Social Research Training Centre for Islamic Countries, Organization of the Islamic Conference, www.sesrtcic.org/stat_database.php (accessed April 16, 2008).

86. "Strategy Document to Enhance the Contribution of an Efficient and Competitive SME Sector to Industrial and Economic Development in Iran," United Nations Industrial Development Organization, 2003, 39.

evidence suggests that China has become the most significant external economic actor in Iran as well as in energy infrastructure.

Conversely, though, Iran is a significant actor in the economy of the Persian Gulf; in particular, Dubai is said to house at least $15 billion in Iranian investment, as well as four hundred thousand expatriate Iranians and nine thousand firms with some Iranian ownership.[87] Iran has also worked assiduously to adopt the Dubai model by opening a profusion of free-trade zones, generally situating them near international borders in hopes of capitalizing on regional trade patterns; however, most are not considered particularly successful in generating new investment or promoting Iranian exports.[88] Iran also has developed a considerable stake in a number of Central Asian countries, supporting major infrastructure projects and helping to found the Economic Cooperation Organization, composed of Iran, Turkey, Pakistan, Azerbaijan, Turkmenistan, Kyrgyzstan, Uzbekistan, Kazakhstan, Tajikistan, and Afghanistan.

One way to assess the relevance of religious identity to Iran's foreign economic policies is to consider recent history. The impact of the oil boom over the past five years on Iran's relationship with the Muslim world is somewhat ambiguous. On the one hand, it is indisputable that Iran's massive oil revenues have emboldened its regime and effectively enabled Ahmadinejad to alienate its traditional trading partners and incur the disapprobation of international institutions such as the United Nations and the Group of Eight (G8) with little concern for the consequences. As an international oil analyst commented, "Right now, the Iranians are in a strong position and they know it. The tight market and high prices provide them not only with a shield but with the high cards. It gives them leverage they didn't have a couple of years ago."[89]

In specific areas of intense Iranian interest, Tehran has expanded its economic ties as vehicles of indirect influence as well as profit. As one analysis noted, "Iran is increasingly spending its oil money in a variety of countries to realize its self-image as an ascendant regional power . . . by focusing on high-profile construction projects, diplomacy, and public relations, Iran was, in effect, employing American cold-war tactics to increase its soft power in the region."[90] Signs along the Afghan highway built by Tehran feature Koranic inscriptions; billboards in Lebanon express gratitude for Iran's largesse; hospitals and medical care for wounded Iraqis and Palestinians are potent vehicles for the Islamic Republic's public diplomacy.

87. "Trade with Dubai Expanding," *Iran Daily*, September 12, 2004; "Friendlier Hands across the Gulf," *Economist*, December 19, 2007, www.economist.com/world/africa/displaystory.cfm?story_id=10328285 (accessed April 16,2008).

88. Earlier this year the Iranian Ministry of Commerce rejected calls to ban reexports from Dubai in order to boost the competitiveness of Iran's free trade zones. "Iran, UAE to Review Investment, Trade Ties," Iranian Republic News Agency, May 15, 2005.

89. Christopher Dickey, "The Oil Shield," *Foreign Policy* (May–June 2006).

90. David Rohde, "Iran Is Seeking More Influence in Afghanistan," *New York Times*, December 27, 2006.

Across the board, however, it is hardly evident that Iran has specifically sought to use its windfall to enhance its position specifically within the Islamic world through a more robust economic relationship or increased foreign assistance. In several cases, Iran has expanded its economic ties to specific Muslim countries simply by virtue of the transformation in the strategic environment; as detailed above, Iran's investments in both Iraq and Afghanistan have mushroomed since the advent of more friendly governments in both countries following U.S. military interventions.

Since Ahmadinejad came into office, Iran has diversified its economic ties in ways that suggest a combination of ideology, opportunism, and anti-Americanism is more significant than religious affiliation. The first two factors help explain the most important dimension of Iran's shifting international economic relations—one that generally is not directed at the Islamic world, but rather geographically oriented toward the east. As they reconsolidated their grip on power over the past several years, a number of prominent Iranian conservatives suggested that an "eastern orientation" would better serve Iran's national interests than its traditional focus on the West. They believed that there were complementary interests between Iran and the expanding new economies of Asia, particularly China and India, and recognized that strengthened economic relations with these regional powers could serve Iran's diplomatic interests. "There are big states in the Eastern Hemisphere such as Russia, China, and India," Larijani said in 2005. "These states can play a balancing role in today's world."[91]

This view is in part the product of a burgeoning relationship between China and Iran since Khomeini's death, which in turn has helped create a "constituency in government, business, and industry—and to some extent in society as well—with vested interests in the advancement of the Sino-Iranian relationship."[92] Ahmadinejad—whose extremely limited foreign experience prior to assuming the presidency included a trip to China—is part of that constituency.

In this respect, Tehran has taken advantage of the rapidly growing Chinese economy and interconnected mercantilist policy of seeking to enhance its involvement with major oil producing countries. Trade between China and Iran is projected to double from its 2004 volume of $7 billion within the decade, with Beijing now just behind Germany in terms of export volumes to Iran.[93] China is now a major actor in the Iranian energy sector, with several

91. Ray Takeyh, "Iran: Assessing Geopolitical Dynamics and U.S. Policy Options," testimony prepared for House Committee on Armed Services, www.cfr.org/publication/10882/iran.html (accessed April 16, 2008).

92. John Calabrese, *China and Iran: Mismatched Partners* (Jamestown Foundation, Occasional Paper, August 2006), 6.

93. Najmeh Bozorgmehr, "Iranian Traders Feel the Lure of Eastern Promise," *Financial Times* (London), September 14, 2007.

long-term liquefied natural gas contracts that also give the Chinese a stake in the development of several untapped Iranian resources, such as the Yadvaran gas field. "China and Iran are perfectly matched for each other," Ali Akbar Vahidi Ale-Agha, an Iranian oil official, said. "China has the world's biggest market of customers and no secure resource for energy. We have a lot of energy, and we need foreign currency. And they have a lot of money to invest. It's a win-win situation."[94] Similar trends apply to Iranian trade with India, which is expected to reach $10 billion annually by 2015 from a mere $3.2 billion in 2004.

The intensifying trade with China and India serves a vital strategic purpose for Tehran. As Iran continued to defy demands from the UN Security Council to suspend its uranium enrichment activities, China became an ever larger factor in shaping the international response to Iran, and its reluctance to ratchet up pressure on Tehran no doubt was informed by its economic stake. Moreover, Iran's turn toward the east has been reinforced by the growing aversion of European companies to Iran as tensions over the nuclear issue mounted, and by the role of U.S. financial restrictions and UN sanctions in further deterring many of Iran's historic trade partners. "We have no choice but to look at the east," observed Habibollah Asgarowladi, an influential Iranian politician with ties to the traditional merchant class. "[O]ur factories are dependent on their technology. But what else can we do when they turn their back on us and bow to U.S. pressure."[95] Frictions between Iran and the West have opened up new opportunities for Russia as well as Asian countries, including Malaysia and Indonesia, whose state-owned oil companies are well-positioned to benefit from the restraint of some of the major European firms.

Beyond taking advantage of the rise of Asian economies and political power, it is clear that Ahmadinejad has taken advantage of Iran's windfall oil revenues to bolster ties to the small array of foreign capitals that share his radical anti-Americanism. He has made several visits to Latin America where he has offered development assistance and hundreds of millions of dollars in investment to Nicaragua and established a $2 billion joint investment fund with Venezuela, no doubt in part due to their leaders' like-minded antipathies toward Washington.[96] A deal signed in October 2007 would ostensibly supply as much as $1 billion per year of Iran's relatively limited gas supplies to Syria beginning in 2009.[97] Finally, Iran can credit Ahmadinejad's

94. Vivienne Walt, "Iran Looks East," *Fortune*, February 21, 2005.

95. Bozorgmehr, "Iranian Traders."

96. Joseph Contreras, "Iran's Foray into Latin America," *Newsweek International*, February 5, 2007; Brian Ellsworth, "Latin America Warms to Iran amid anti-U.S. Sentiment," Reuters, August 29, 2007.

97. "Tehran, Damascus Ink Gas Deal Worth $1 Billion a Year," Agence France-Presse, October 5, 2007.

active economic diplomacy with securing investment from Belarus in its oil sector—a move of dubious utility. The overall record of recent years has provoked intense skepticism from the Iranian president's critics. In surveying Ahmadinejad's forty-one foreign trips—a rate of one every nineteen days—during his first two and one-half years in office, a reformist newspaper expressed incredulity. "Given the fact that Mr. Ahmadinejad's election pledges in the presidential election were economic and in relation to securing bread and water for the people as well as fighting inflation and surging prices, which of these trips have had an economic aspect?"[98]

Iran's economic interests have not always proven to be a force of cohesion in the wider Islamic world; rather, they have frequently triggered or exacerbated frictions, particularly between Iran and its neighbors. As two of OPEC's heavyweights—but with vastly different production profiles and reserves—Iran and Saudi Arabia have historically clashed on oil production and pricing policies. As recently as 1998—two years after the slow thaw between Riyadh and Tehran commenced—the hard-line Iranian newspaper *Jomhuri-ye Eslami* opined that Saudi Arabia was to blame for OPEC's inability to stanch the drop in oil prices. "The Saudis must be addressed with the strongest of sentences and the clearest of screams," the editorial demanded. "The finger of accusation must identify them as the element in this great and historic treason to their own people and to the other nations of the OPEC countries."[99] However, as pressures on the Saudi budget intensified during the 1990s and early part of this decade, both governments appear to have made a strategic decision in the mid-1990s that addressing their shared economic priorities could provide a platform for an enduring rapprochement. Together with the advent of the reform movement in Iran, this convergence of interests enabled Riyadh and Tehran to cooperate in setting OPEC quotas and policy. Close coordination between the Saudis and the Iranians within OPEC helped facilitate the recovery of oil prices from their late 1990s low. As a variety of factors—most importantly, epic growth and energy demand in China and India—pushed the price of oil beyond $120 a barrel, Riyadh and Tehran found even greater grounds for cooperation in this arena, despite the regressions in Iran's internal situation.

There are a number of other areas where Iran's economic interests have initiated or exacerbated frictions with the broader Muslim world. This is particularly the case with respect to the exploitation of resources in the Caspian Sea. Since the collapse of the Soviet Union, Iran has continued to contest vigorously the legal framework for the Caspian Sea, asserting it has a right to 20 percent of the Caspian surface area and sea bed, and has argued

---

98. "A Look at Ahmadinejad's 41 Foreign Trips," Badrossadat Mofidi, *Etemad*, December 24, 2007, www.etemaad.com/Released/86-10-03/204.htm#60443 (accessed May 9, 2008).

99. "Paper on Saudi Oil 'Treason,' US Visitors Tehran," *Jomhuri-ye Eslami*, December 3, 1998.

repeatedly that the "unresolved" status of the region should preclude any exploitation of the petroleum resources within it. This position has sparked direct and ongoing conflict with Azerbaijan in particular. In 2001, Iran deployed a gunboat to intimidate two Azeri survey ships (operated by British Petroleum), effectively halting efforts to explore and develop the Alov field.

The Russians initially flirted with the Iranian position but in later years signed bilateral and trilateral treaties with Kazakhstan and Azerbaijan that will at least permit economic development of the northern Caspian. (It left some of the issues concerning sovereignty unresolved.) The May 2003 agreement divided the northern two-thirds of the sea into three unequal parts, with Kazakhstan receiving control of 27 percent, Russia 19 percent, and Azerbaijan 18 percent. Iran continues to argue that any agreement on the Caspian must include all five littoral states to be legally binding and regularly convenes a "working group" composed of representatives of the littoral states. Given the aggressive nationalism that the Islamic Republic has injected into this issue, this dispute is likely to remain unresolved and continue to generate friction between Iran and its neighbors.

Control of resources along the border has also sparked tensions between Iran and Kuwait. In early 2000, Iran began drilling in the Dorra field, located in a contested region of the northern Gulf continental shelf. After sharp rebukes from Kuwait, Iran withdrew its drilling rigs. In July 2000, Saudi Arabia and Kuwait agreed to divide the field equally, and since that time Kuwait has taken the lead on trying to wrest some sort of accommodation with Tehran, with little success. Moreover, it remains to be seen how the Islamic Republic will respond to new efforts by its Gulf neighbors to enforce UN economic sanctions on Iran and adhere to U.S. restrictions on interactions with several Iranian banks. As of December 2007, several of Iran's key Gulf trade partners had begun to enforce the restrictions, further complicating international business dealings for Iranian companies and individuals.[100]

Finally, the resurgence of hard-line ideologues within Iran's ministries and bureaucracies is likely to generate new instances of discord over foreign investment in key sectors of the economy, even when that investment comes from the broader Muslim world. In May 2004, the Revolutionary Guards blocked the opening of the new Imam Khomeini International Airport south of Tehran on the grounds that a Turkish-Austrian firm had been selected to manage the new facility. The uproar also resulted in revision to another potential Turkish investment—a $366 million mobile phone deal—after the younger generation of conservatives who dominate the parliament demanded modifications.

100.Steven Mufson and Robin Wright, "Iran Adapts to Economic Pressure," *Washington Post*, October 29, 2007.

Iran the Model: Religious Institutions and Cultural Influence

Since its inception, the Islamic Republic of Iran has always recognized the power of cultural influence. The roots of its involvement with terrorism trace back to its establishment of a variety of organizations and institutions intended to promote the "export of the revolution" to the broader Muslim world. It is important to note that Iran's interest in those early days was not focused on those regions or countries where it might draw particularly on Persian influence or Shia communities; at its outset, the Islamic Revolution was envisioned by its most orthodox proponents as a universalist phenomenon.

While most attention has focused on Iran's use of subversion and terrorism to "export the revolution," it is important to recognize that at least in public statements, Khomeini conceived of this very much in cultural, nonviolent terms, decrying the use of "swords" on multiple occasions as an instrument for power projection. For the Islamic Republic's founder, the most effective way to export its revolutionary fervor was through the dissemination of its precepts and the advocacy of its officials, citizenry, and a broader network of clergy. Khomeini told Iranian athletes that "our way of exporting Islam is through the youth who go to other countries where a large number of people come to see you and your achievements. You must behave in such a way that these large gatherings are attracted to Islam by your action. Your deeds, your action, and your behavior should be an example, and through you the Islamic Republic will go to other places, God willing."[101]

This view helped inform Iran's embrace of Islamic themes in its diplomacy and its determination to promote its views and its place in the Islamic order, through controversy and provocation where necessary. The Islamic Republic routinely used the hajj as political theater, an unparalleled opportunity to advance its claims to leadership of the Islamic world, radicalize other Muslims, and discomfit Saudi authorities by pitting their own aspirations to communal leadership against their paramount interest in retaining their American security alliance. Coordinated by the same cleric who had served as the spiritual leader of the students who took over the American Embassy in 1979, Iran's pilgrims routinely rallied against Washington as well as the Saudi regime. In several years, the animosities sparked by Iran's agitation and the Saudi response contributed to violent clashes and disasters.[102]

---

101. Ramazani, *Revolutionary Iran*, 26.
102. Henner Furtig, *Iran's Rivalry with Saudi Arabia between the Gulf Wars* (Ithaca, NY: Cornell University Press, 2002), 42–55.

While the hajj provided a predictable annual forum for Iranian agitprop, in other cases Iranian authorities took advantage of opportunities as they presented themselves, such as the 1989 publication of Salman Rushdie's novel *The Satanic Verses* and the 2006 controversy over an op-ed cartoon published in a Danish newspaper. In both cases, Tehran picked up on opposition voiced by clerics and Islamist political figures outside Iran, in Pakistan and in Europe, respectively. But each time, Iranian authorities positioned themselves as the most fervent champion of Muslim sanctities and sentiments. While this earned the opprobrium of the West and in some cases other Islamic leaders, the echo from Arab and Muslim populations provided a boost that Tehran obviously valued.

Iran's deployment of anti-Israeli rhetoric deserves special attention. Obviously, Iranian leaders have a long and ignominious history of seeking to shore up their credentials as purported leaders of the Islamic world by invoking the Palestinian cause and aligning themselves with the most virulent strands of opposition to Israel. For their part, of course, Israeli politicians have also indulged in extravagant denunciations of Iran and its policies. Khomeini spared little civility in his discourse on Israel, and Khamenei, in responding to news of Yitzhak Rabin's 1995 assassination, dismissed Israel as a "false and artificial" entity and opened a 2001 conference on the Palestinian intifada by calling for Israel's "annihilation."[103] It is important to note that during the Khatami presidency, the reformist movement contributed to a meaningful shift in Iran's debate on its approach to Israel through public questioning of the revolution's ideological verities by key officials and influential newspapers. However, many of the reformists remained passionately anti-Israeli, the legacy of the faction's evolution from the radical left wing, and even as Khatami signaled that Iran would abide by any peace that was accepted by the Palestinians, some of his closest domestic advisers were among the most virulent on the subject of Israel's existence.[104]

Still, even within this historical context, Ahmadinejad managed to up the ante, galvanize international outrage, and produce unprecedented international consensus on the need to isolate Iran. He began in October 2005 by reviving one of Khomeini's notable invectives toward Israel, proclaiming that the Jewish state must be erased from the pages of history. Then, at the December 2005 OIC summit, Ahmadinejad went a step further, calling for Israel to be moved to Europe and voicing skepticism about the Holocaust, presumably as a way of irritating his Saudi hosts and claiming the mantle of leadership of the Islamic world. A week later, Ahmadinejad described the

---

103. Parsi, *Treacherous Alliance*, 192; Guy Dinmore, "Conference in Iran Calls for Israel's Destruction," *Financial Times* (London), April 25, 2001.

104. Most notable is Ali Akbar Mohtashamipur, who can be credited with playing a key role both in the operational establishment of Hezbollah as well as in the ideological framing of the reformist critique of Iran's Islamic system.

Holocaust as a "myth" before a domestic audience,[105] and in December 2006, the Foreign Ministry's think tank—once the most popular venue for American policy analysts to visit Iran—hosted a conference to "investigate" the historical reality of the Holocaust.

The remarks caused a sensation, prompting widespread condemnation of the Iranian president from nearly every world leader. At home, there were several official efforts to "spin" Ahmadinejad's comments, while several Iranian politicians, including Khatami, explicitly challenged Ahmadinejad's views, and others objected publicly to the damage to Iran's interests wrought by the controversy.[106] Even among the conservative stalwarts of the regime, there was a sense that the president had overplayed the Israel card and the conservative parliament eventually grilled his foreign minister over the issue.

But the issue, and the explosive attention that it received, also ingratiated Ahmadinejad with two critical constituencies—Iran's hard-line power brokers and popular opinion across the Arab and Muslim world. Khamenei immediately endorsed Ahmadinejad's views on Israel, as did a number of Iranian parliamentarians and hard-line clerics. The conservative newspaper *Keyhan* saw the episode as a long-overdue resumption of a critical but neglected element of Iran's foreign policy, the export of the revolution, without which Iran would inevitably find itself on the defensive. "If the competitor hides in the corner of the ring without recognizing its abilities," *Keyhan* advised, "he will get nothing but a good beating."[107]

Beyond Iran, the invective served its purpose—anecdotal evidence suggested that the president of Iran's Shia theocracy suddenly had become one of the most popular figures among many Arabs and Muslims. Ahmadinejad exalted in his new popularity, proclaiming that "the world of humanity is on the threshold of a major and fundamental transformation today. You can see the consequences of this transformation wherever you visit in the world. A couple of days ago, when we were in Riyadh to attend the OPEC conference . . . inside the conference hall, young people wearing Arabic attire would come to see us. They used to clench their fists with enthusiasm and with a certain degree of excitement and thrill would yell: 'Long live Iran; We love Iran; We follow Iran's model; We are prepared to sacrifice our lives for Iran.'"[108] Ahmadinejad took

---

105. President Mahmoud Ahmadinejad, speech in Zahedan on December 14, 2005, broadcast on Islamic Republic of Iran News Network, translated by BBC Monitoring.

106. "Iran Official: President's Holocaust Remarks 'Misunderstood,'" Associated Press, December 16, 2005; "Former Iran President Says Holocaust Is a 'Fact,'" Reuters, September 9, 2005; Ali Akbar Dareini, "Ex-Nuke Envoy Raps Ahmadinejad Policies," Associated Press, October 10, 2007; "Iran not Seeking Israel Destruction: Larijani," Agence France-Presse, May 18, 2007.

107. Naser Bahramirad, "Foreign Policy: Active or Inactive?" *Keyhan*, December 20, 2005.

108. President Mahmoud Ahmadinejad, speech in Ardabil Province, broadcast on Vision of the Islamic Republic of Iran Ardabil Provincial TV on November 23, 2007, World News Connection.

his cues from the response and has repeatedly reinjected these themes into his discourse throughout the course of his presidency.

Beyond its rhetorical posturing toward Israel, the Iranian government has always placed a premium on what has come to be known as "public diplomacy" for enhancing its legitimacy at home as well as promoting its vision abroad. Internally, the regime maintains a monopoly over broadcasting—satellites though prolific remain technically illegal—and oversight of the Islamic Republic of Iran Broadcasting (IRIB) organization has always been entrusted to allies of the senior leadership. IRIB broadcasts in a number of regional languages, particularly Arabic, and in 2007 launched an English-language station known as Press TV.

Another important vehicle is the Organization for the Propagation of Islam (Sazeman-e Tablighat-e Eslami) or IPO. The IPO is headed by hard-line cleric Hojatoleslam Mohammad Mohammadi-Araqi and continues to organize a range of politico-religious activities both within Iran as well as in other Islamic countries, including the routine revolutionary rallies denouncing Israel and the United States. In Iran, the IPO's most notable achievement in recent years was the publication of *Entekhab*, a conservative newspaper that for five years until its closure last year managed to transcend some of the faction's rigidities and articulate a modernist defense of the Islamic Republic. The IPO continues to publish the far less innovative English-language *Tehran Times*, as well as the Mehr News Agency, a Web site oriented toward promoting a hard-line spin on news, which publishes in Persian, English, Arabic, Turkish, Urdu, and German.

With regard to official Iranian public diplomacy, here too Ahmadinejad has broken new ground, with his habit of penning personal letters to various world leaders as well as the American public. While there is little evidence to suggest that this has achieved significant results for Iran, it speaks to the president's recognition that publicity surrounding the Islamic Republic and its officials, views, and policies can be a valuable asset in the country's efforts to assert itself on the world stage. On this basis, Ahmadinejad's bravura performances at the annual UN General Assembly meeting and his active courting of public speaking engagements and the American media on his visits to New York reflect a broader strategy of extending Iran's influence that has some resonance.

In similar fashion, the Islamic Republic has also cultivated a network of sympathetic followers through a variety of religiously inspired parastatal institutions that have international reach. For example, the Komiteh-ye Emdad-e Imam (Imam's Relief Committee) engages in international development work and disaster relief assistance in neighboring countries such as Azerbaijan, Tajikistan, and Afghanistan, but also coordinated emergency relief supplies for Kosovar Muslims and is a major conduit for assistance to southern Lebanon. The Bonyad-e Shahid (Martyrs' Foundation)—set up to service families of the victims of the revolution and later the Iraq war—has also expanded its activities overseas, establishing affiliated organizations in Lebanon and elsewhere. Tehran's efforts to fund mosques and promote educational curricula that support Iran's unique system of religious rule and other elements of Iranian Shia culture are considerably smaller than the vast Wahhabi outreach undertaken by the Saudi government, but they nonetheless constitute a source of influence for the Islamic Republic. In Kashmir, Iranian-supported institutions promoted Khomeini's philosophy to the point of conflict with indigenous Shia mosques; they also engaged in political patronage.[109]

In the longer term, however, Iran's greater influence on the wider Shia world may come through its doctrinal and institutional innovations. One of the many misconceptions surrounding the Islamic government is the assumption of essentialism with regard to the nature of the clergy. Rhetoric from Tehran has no doubt cultivated such imagery. In reality, however, the traditional hierarchy of Iranian Shiism has not remained static; considerable evolution took place, particularly in the eighteenth century when a fierce doctrinal battle took place. The conflict divided the clergy between advocates of clerical intercession and interpretation (loosely referred to as the Usuli school of Shia jurisprudence) and traditionalists who maintained that the sacred texts provided sufficient guidance for individual believers (the Akhbari school). The triumph of the Usulis over the Akhbaris can be considered "the cornerstone of contemporary Shia theology"[110] and one of the key elements that distinguishes religious thought and practice in Iran. In fact, Usuli doctrine and concepts provided the underpinnings of the clerical arguments in support of Iran's Constitutional Revolution.[111]

Under the Islamic Republic, this principle has been taken several steps further. Despite the state's efforts to centralize and systematize Islam, as discussed below, Iran's seminaries have in fact fostered a tremendous amount of intellectual and doctrinal ferment. One of the most interesting developments has been the articulation and exploration of dynamic jurisprudence (*fiqh-e puya*). Led by the diverse but convergent writings of philosopher Abdolkarim Soroush and clerics Mohammad Mojtahed-Shabestari and Mohsen Kadivar, proponents of dynamic jurisprudence, argue that religious knowledge is changing, incomplete, and pluralistic and see the concomitant need for the clergy to incorporate man's ever-evolving knowledge and experience in nonreligious affairs. These doctrinal innova-

---

109. Cameron W. Barr, "To Highly Tense Kashmir, Add Iranian-Style Islam," *Christian Science Monitor*, June 26, 1998.

110. Shahrough Akhavi, *Religion and Politics in Contemporary Iran: Clergy-State Relations in the Pahlavi Period* (Albany: State University of New York Press, 1980), 121.

111. Hamid Enayat, *Modern Islamic Political Thought* (Austin: University of Texas Press, 1982), 121. The 1905 Constitutional Revolution represents Iran's first modern attempt to institutionalize representative rule. As Enayat commented, "The political implications of these principles can hardly be overstated. By upholding the authority of reason and the right *ijtihad*, the *Usuli* doctrines could not fail to render the Shi'i mind susceptible to social changes."

tions represent an intellectual dissent against the political and theological implications of the way that power has been organized in the Islamic Republic—and each of the three thinkers above has paid the price via prison or hard-liner harassment.

Prior to the Islamic Revolution, the endorsement of clerical interpretation (or *ijtihad*) of religious traditions and doctrines engrained a limited range of functional pluralism within the clerical hierarchy—a diversity which was openly accepted until the clerical accession to formal power after the Islamic Revolution. Moreover, the empowerment of individual clerics to interpret holy law enhanced the social value and prominence of their role, which resulted in the consolidation of authority and the empowerment of the institution of *marja-ye taqlid*, or source of emulation. These networks were closely intertwined with the merchant community, as well as with the landed classes (which many senior clergy would be considered a part of by virtue of their *vaqf* endowments).[112] But while they shared important social bonds and an overarching opposition to the monarchy's repressive policies toward the religious establishment, the clergy themselves were by no means coherently unified either prior to, or in the aftermath of, the revolution itself. This diversity in fact derives from the traditionally polycephalic structure of Shiism.

This structure implies that the clerical networks represent a complicated challenge for integration within a bureaucratized system of power. First, they are inherently informal, personalized, and small-scale; a cleric advances not through a discrete selection process or a finite set of criteria, but through the recognition and assent of his peers, who at the highest levels would typically consist of fewer than one hundred fellow ayatollahs and several hundred other close associates. This structure implies that "the respective networks formed by each source of imitation and his following were organizationally, financially, and ideologically independent of one another."[113] Second, the role of the *marja*s generates a multiplicity of authorities; the relatively late development of the concept of preeminence (via the evolution of this role of the "source of emulation") evidences a "strong juridical preference for a collective leadership that allows a degree of *ekhtelaf*, divergence of opinion in legal matters not directly concerned with the basic principles of religion or with fundamental aspects of dogma."[114]

In the aftermath of the doctrinal decision in favor of individual interpretation, the clergy faced a relatively weak ruling dynasty and thus expanded

---

112. Homa Omid, *Islam and the Post-Revolutionary State in Iran* (New York: St. Martin's Press, 1994), 43. By one account, in the immediate prerevolutionary period, all seven marja-ye taqlid shared kinship and other linkages with the bazaaris and landlords.

113. Guilain Denoeux, *Urban Unrest in the Middle East: Comparative Study of Informal Networks in Egypt, Iran, and Lebanon* (Albany: State University of New York Press, 1993), 163.

114. Mangol Bayat, "Shia Islam as a Functioning Ideology in Iran: The Cult of the Hidden Imam," in *Iran Since the Revolution: Internal Dynamics, Regional Conflict, and the Superpowers*, ed. Barry Rosen (New York: Columbia University Press, 1985), 22.

rapidly, depleting any sense of institutional identity and coherence and encouraging stratification at the highest ranks of the clergy. For the first time,
one individual (Ayatollah Murtada Ansari, died 1864) assumed the role of
the single source of emulation (*marja-ye taqlid-e motlaq*) for all Shia believers
around the world. The middle and lower ranks of the clerical hierarchy remained amorphous and lacking in any organizational rules or structure to
coordinate jurisprudence.[115] This lack of organization left the religious ranks
profoundly vulnerable to state encroachment, and the policies of state building and consolidation adopted by the Pahlavi monarchs engendered a sense
of siege among the clergy, who viewed the establishment of civil authority
over law making and enforcement, education, and the religious infrastructure of mosques and endowments as an existential threat.

As a result, one might expect that once they had assumed power, the
clergy would seek to strengthen these institutions and to make full use
of these alliances and resources, because of their compelling interest in
protecting their traditional bases of authority, which remained instru-
mentally effective in securing their political position. Their pursuit of
such a policy, however, was somewhat ambiguous, and this ambiguity
has reduced the overall efficacy of the Islamic state. In some cases, the
clerics in power attempted to create new bureaucratic channels to utilize
religious rhetoric to mobilize support for the new regime; this of course
would strengthen the state's symbolic mandate. One of the important
steps in this process was the establishment of a centralized structure for
Friday prayers. Throughout the modern history of Iran, the Friday prayer
sermons had served as a barometer of the relative degree of autonomy
between the state and the religious hierarchy.[116] The Islamic Republic's
leadership uses their appointment of prayer leaders (*imam jomehs*) as a potent vehicle for transmitting a unified political message through a medium
that invokes great respect. "Since 1979, the Friday prayer sermon has been
vigorously revived, and fully institutionalized as one of the main pillars
of the theocratic state."[117] In late 1983, the government established a formal
organization for the Friday prayer leaders to provide centralized oversight
and serve as a vehicle for mobilization; the original proposal also entailed

---

115. Said Amir Arjomand, *The Shadow of God and the Hidden Imam: Religion, Political Order, and
Societal Change in Shi'ite Iran from the Beginning to 1980* (Chicago: University of Chicago
Press, 1984), 245-47.

116. During the Safavid era, the *ulema* utilized their sermons to endorse the dynasty; later, the
Friday sermon emerged as a potent voice for clerical opposition to government policy,
particularly during the Constitutional Revolution. The Pahlavis appointed Friday prayer
leaders largely on grounds of political reliability, which deprived them of an effective role
in either state legitimation or opposition. See Haggay Ram, *Myth and Mobilization in Revolutionary Iran: The Use of the Friday Congregational Sermon* (Washington, DC: American University Press, 1994), 22–23.

117. "Iran's Islamic Fundamentalism and Terrorism: A View from the Pulpit," *Studies in Conflict
and Terrorism* 12, no. 6 (1989): 401.

integrating the imam jomehs within the intelligence-gathering networks, with an eye toward one day delegating responsibility for all provincial and local administrative affairs to this bureaucracy as well.[118]

In fact, the network of Friday prayer leaders eventually emerged as the regime's main instrument for disseminating and instilling the official ideology with the public, and it was so effective that it contributed to the sidelining of the less effective Islamic Republican Party. Thus, contrary to many other Muslim countries, today in Iran Friday prayers are centralized, civic events coordinated by institutions of the national government; the service has become a rather stage-managed spectacle and sermons focus heavily on national and international issues. This rejection of "the party in favor of the mosque [controlled by the imam jomeh] as the organ of communal unity and mobilization" attests to the deliberate attempt to employ traditional institutions in the modern structure of the state under the Islamic Republic.[119]

This enduring conflict between the parliament and its supervisory body, the Guardians' Council, prompted an extraordinary ruling by Ayatollah Khomeini in January 1988, elevating the *velayet-e faqih* above "all ordinances that were derived or directly commanded by Allah."[120] A month later, he institutionalized this principle through the establishment of the Council for Assessing the Interests of the System (Majma-ye Tashkhis-e Maslahat-e Nezam), or the Expediency Council. This organization was tasked with mediating between the parliament and the Guardians' Council on disputed legislation, as well as introducing independent legislation, and it is empowered to override both the Constitution and sharia in order to frame decisions that it deems in the best interests of the Islamic state. Its membership (who serve five-year terms) includes the heads of the three divisions of government, the six clerics on the Council of Guardians, and relevant cabinet ministers, as well as others appointed by the faqih.

The principle invoked by the establishment of this council was not a new one; in fact, it was evidenced in Khomeini's earliest conceptualization of Islamic government, in which he advances the somewhat vague injunction of "protecting Islam" over prayers or fasting (two of the five basic imperatives of the Muslim faith).[121] Indeed, this precept (*maslehat*) had served as the basis for numerous Guardians' Council decisions during the revolution's first decade, and the establishment of a body specifically tasked with regularizing this

118. Said Amir Arjomand, *The Turban for the Crown: The Islamic Revolution in Iran* (New York and Oxford: Oxford University Press, 1988), 167–69.

119. Ibid.

120. Asghar Schirazi, *The Constitution of Iran Politics and the State in the Islamic Republic* (London: I.B. Tauris, 1997), 64.

121. Hamid Enayat, "Iran: Khumayni's Concept of the 'Guardianship of the Jurisconsult,'" in *Islam in the Political Process*, ed. James Piscatori (Cambridge: Cambridge University Press, 1983), 170.

principle represented "simply the official sanctioning of a practice which had been recognized for some time and which was now supplemented by the creation of a formal institution."[122]

The ruling also empowered further institutionalization of the Islamic Republic as an entity distinct from, and competitive with, traditional networks of religious authority in Iran. The Expediency Council was expanded and empowered in 1997, in preparation for its assumption by then president Hashemi Rafsanjani;[123] from these changes, and from Rafsanjani's own conduct since that time, it is apparent that the Council was intended to serve as a vehicle for his personal political ambitions, as well as the further distancing of the Iranian state from theological bases.[124] While the Expediency Council remains a crucial body for determining the ultimate nature of the government's agenda, it is also clear from the parliamentary elections that the burden of popular expectations—and the credit or blame that accompany those—fall largely on the popularly elected Majlis rather than on the rather shrouded decision making of the Expediency Council.

The acknowledgment of the primacy of national interest, as well as similar rulings that enhanced the authority of the velayet-e faqih, can be interpreted merely as acknowledgments of the secular, political incentives that are paramount in Islamic Iran. This pragmatic basis for state action has certainly facilitated the perpetuation of the Islamic regime, but it has also established problematic precedents for the country's traditional Shia institutions and for the tenacity of the Islamic state. The importation of an essentially Sunni precept, and the degrading of sharia may contribute to the development of a more flexible legal system in Iran, one that incorporates Islam but is not hostage to antiquated interpretations. In fact, the attempt to tie Islamic law to daily governance through maneuvers such as the adoption of maslehat may actually freeze religious thought and diminish the tendency of Islamic jurisprudence in Iran to support pluralistic interpretations.[125] Moreover, by empowering an Islamic critique of the state and exposing the fragility of the state's genuine religious legitimacy, the ruling leaves the state vulnerable to exactly the sort of challenge that created it. The invocation of maslehat "was

---

122. Schirazi, *The Constitution of Iran*, 237.

123. Olivier Roy, "Tensions in Iran: The Future of the Islamic Revolution," *Middle East Report* (Summer 1998): 40.

124. This effort appears to have foundered somewhat; the former president found himself under a vicious attack from reformers in his campaign for a seat in the parliament in which he once served as speaker, and in the end, he fared quite poorly in the February 2000 Majlis elections.

125. Given the prerogative of continual interpretation in Shia Islam, such an innovation is unnecessary. This of course encapsulates in a highly simplified manner one of the strains of the argument today in Iran over the future of Islamic law and philosophy, most prominently articulated by the renowned Iranian dissident Abdolkarim Soroush. For background on the underpinnings of this debate, see Mehrzad Boroujerdi, *Iranian Intellectuals and the West: A Study in Orientalism in Reverse* (Albany: State University of New York Press, 1992).

meant as a doctrinal vindication for *raison d'etat*, but was nonetheless quite incongruous coming from a man who had made his career criticizing secular rulers for disregarding divine law. Khomeini thus undermined the very foundations of the theocracy he had hoped to establish in Iran."[126]

In fact, the central institution of this ostensible theocracy—the velayet-e faqih—has also established a somewhat problematic legacy for the broader Muslim world. At first appraisal, the creation of a formal office of the faqih appears to represent merely the formalization of Khomeini's personal charismatic authority and thus in its initial stages seemed to impose only minimal structural change in the patterns and institutions of the ulema. However, the evolution of this office under both Khomeini and his successor Khamenei dramatizes the way in which the continuing contestation among rival groups has generated dramatic changes in the nature and structure of religious authority in Iran—and by extension, for the broader Shia community. This represents the continuation of a process begun during the mobilization of the clergy as a segment—in fact, the leading segment—of the anti-Shah movement, which necessitated first a fundamental ideational conversion toward embracing a political role. The transfer of religious authority to the state has entailed increasing bureaucratization and absolutism for the state, and growing politicization for religion. Politics in Iran today is now imbued with the sanctity of the divine, while religion has been tainted by the expediency of political prerequisites.

This development became most evident as the state began to shed the personalism of its beginnings. The issue of identifying an individual or individuals to fulfill the responsibilities of the velayet-e faqih loomed large in the Islamic Republic, even in the early construction of the state. The handling of the succession issue over the past twenty years has contributed to the increasing absolutism of the Islamic system, the devolution of the traditional patterns of consensus and meritocratic authority among the Iranian clergy, and a singular uncomfortable paradox—the man who was once tapped to succeed Khomeini as faqih, Ayatollah Hussein Ali Montazeri, is today one of the most prominent critics of the system. His 1989 dismissal and the subsequent elevation of Ali Khamenei to the position of leader has further politicized the process and nature of clerical stature, and thereby weakened the historically consensual and meritocratic clergy.

At the time of his promotion, Khamenei was considered a *hojjatoleslam*, literally "proof of Islam," which represents "the most widely held rank for graduates of theological seminaries, held by approximately twenty-eight thousand people in Iran." His elevation as faqih also earned him a notch up the religious ranks, as the state media began referring to Khamenei as

---

126. H.E. Chehabi, "Religion and Politics in Iran: How Theocratic Is the Islamic Republic?" *Daedalus* 120 (Summer 1991): 81.

"ayatollah" and the designation has stuck.[127] His assumption of the state's highest office was facilitated by the constitutional revisions (which were informally understood at the time of his promotion and ratified shortly thereafter). Based on a letter penned by Khomeini shortly before his death,[128] these revisions downgraded the religious qualifications required of the faqih, explicitly gave preference to political over theological standards in the selection process, and eliminated provisions for delegating the velayet-e faqih to a council of jurists (*fuqaha*) in the event an appropriate individual could not be identified. Thus, after having previously subordinated religious law to state interest, the ostensibly theocratic Islamic Republic formally separated its political leadership from religious leadership.

This separation has empowered the political dimension of leadership at the expense of traditional authority and institutions. Ironically, as its standing within the religious hierarchy has waned, the office of the faqih has actually absorbed greater authority. Having removed the prospect of the guardianship role being borne by a council of clerics, the premise of velayet-e faqih was then progressively centralized to entail the unquestioned leadership of a single individual. In addition, the powers of this individual have been expanded; in several areas where the office has always claimed supervisory power, the faqih now possesses sole jurisdiction, a meaningful supplement to its authority in practice and to the absoluteness with which the office itself is administered. The elimination of the prime ministerial position as part of this revision deprived the state of competing sources of authority, and remanded Iran's parastatal economic foundations, as well as other organizations such as the state broadcasting organization, wholly within the domain of the faqih.[129] More broadly, the constitutional revisions of 1989 explicitly added the faqih's "absolute general trusteeship" over the three branches of government to the powers of this office, in an effort to assist Khomeini's successor in filling his shoes.[130] Finally, in a progressive accretion of its status, Khomeini in 1989 formally elevated the absolute mandate of the jurist to the highest order of divine commandment. "Thus sacralized, the new Shiite political order demands unconditional obedience from the individual as an incumbent religious duty."[131]

---

127. Wilfried Buchta, *Who Rules Iran?* (Washington, DC: The Washington Institute for Near East Policy, 1999): 15; Saskia Gieling, "The *Marja'iya* in Iran and the Nomination of Khamenei in December 1994," *Middle Eastern Studies* 33, no. 4 (October 1997): 778.

128. In the letter, Khomeini claimed, among other things, that he had never supported the requirement of marja status for the holder of the velayet-e faqih, and that it had been forced upon him by others. There is at least some plausibility to this claim, as Khomeini's own status as a marja-ye taqlid was not entirely certain at the time of the revolution. However, Schirazi comments that this "assertion contradicts the relevant passages in Khomeini's book on the Islamic state." Schirazi, *The Constitution of Iran*, 107.

129. Muhammad Sadiq al-Husayni, "Interview with Hashemi Rafsanjani," *Al-Sharq Al-Awsat*, December 19, 1997.

130. Schirazi, *The Constitution of Iran*, 77–78.

131. Arjomand, *The Turban for the Crown*, 182–83.

The superficial pragmatism of these shifts overlooks the significant damage that these instrumental reinterpretations of dogma and reconstructions of clerical authority entail for the Islamic state. The guardianship of the jurist—which constitutes the central premise of the Islamic Republic—rejects the pluralism that is the historic trademark of Shiism, and insists on unity on both political and doctrinal matters. This is a twist of the classical Islamic concept of *towhid*, signifying the unity of God or monotheism; Khomeini "has gradually broadened the concept by insisting that such monotheism encompasses not only the oneness of God but the oneness of the Islamic community and also the one, proper way to realize God's will."[132] As a result, Khomeini's doctrine of velayet-e faqih explicitly establishes a new and separate hierarchy within the Iranian clergy—one that is based on political credentials and adherence to a particular set of policy-related principles, rather than on the traditional criteria of scholarship, piety, and moral integrity.

This new hierarchy differs from the traditional clergy in its rejection of pluralism and the enhancement of centralized power. Khomeini's insistence on doctrinal unity precludes the very autonomy and inherently meritocratic diversity that made the clergy such a durable force in Islamic history. The faqih wields vastly greater powers than the ulema have historically aspired to, including areas of responsibility that were historically the province of secular officials, such as control over all three branches of government and command of the armed forces. The Islamic system also grants the political clergy greater powers over the religious administration than the consensual patterns of clerical decision making had ever sanctioned, including the prerogative to defrock individual *mujtahids*.[133] Besides eclipsing the *marja'iyat* in terms of its responsibilities and capabilities, the replication of the clerical hierarchy through the Islamic system has contributed to the erosion of the authority of the traditional clergy with the unabashed politicization of its traditional networks.

The expansion of the faqih's powers and the sacralization of that authority have been aggressively instituted at every level of Iranian political life. For example, the vetting process for political office has adopted a loyalty test that requires candidates to profess fealty to the institution of velayet-e faqih. This was not a component of the earliest screening of prospective applicants for political office by the Guardians' Council, and appears to

132. Marvin Zonis, "The Rule of the Clerics in the Islamic Republic of Iran," *The Annals of the American Academy of Political and Social Sciences*, no. 482 (November 1985), 96.

133. For example, in April 1982, 17 out of 45 professors within the Qom seminary association voted to "demote" Grand Ayatollah Shariatmadari because of his opposition to velayet-e faqih. Arjomand, *The Turban for the Crown*, 156. In 1987, a separate branch of the judiciary was established and devoted to prosecuting clerical deviations and breaches of the ruling ideology (particularly of velayet-e faqih). Its first case was that of Mehdi Hashemi, who was executed for his role in exposing the arms-for-hostages arrangement between Iran and the United States.

reflect a sort of defensive effort to bolster the adherence to this office within the system. These changes increased the weight of the institution of velayet-e faqih, at the precise moment that its agency had been weakened by Khomeini's inevitable demise. Today, the office of the velayet-e faqih represents ground zero for political contention within the Islamic Republic. President Khatami has described the leadership as a permanent and uncontested fixture on the Iranian political scene: "The idea of velayet-e faqih is no longer just one jurisprudential view alongside others. It is the basis of our political and civil system."[134] At the opposing end of the political spectrum is the increasingly public opposition to the velayet-e faqih from a variety of Iranian clerics, politicians, and journalists, who have compared the proscription on criticism of the faqih and the gradual sanctification of this position with the environment cultivated by the monarchy.[135]

Today, the structure of the office of the faqih, which embodies substantially nonliturgical duties such as command of the armed forces, as well as its administration, have integrated a prominent secular component into the development of the Iranian clergy. By engaging in assiduous cross-institutional patronage and elevating state interests over religious law, both Khomeini and Khamenei have politicized the clerical community and redirected the patterns of its organization. The development of strategic reciprocity between the faqih and key individuals and institutions within the Islamic system has proved a critical element for Khamenei, whose theological stature and personal charisma is far less substantial than that of his predecessor.

The one institution that faqih has not successfully absorbed is that of the traditional position of leadership within the clergy, the marja-ye taqlid (source of emulation). Khamenei's relatively lowly stature in the theological hierarchy created inherent (although somewhat ambiguous) limitations for the authority of that office, and of the state more generally, and perhaps more dangerously, left the state open to rival assertions of religious mandate from clerics with greater theological mandates than Khamenei. This vulnerability was temporarily resolved with the state's acknowledgment of two elderly, and essentially apolitical, senior clerics as marjas after Khomeini's death; their authority was certainly not strong, given their own questionable credentials, but they were largely accepted by the ulema and were unlikely

---

134. Khatami's first address of the formal 1997 presidential campaign, broadcast on Vision of the Islamic Republic Network One, May 10, 1997.

135. Hojjatoleslam Mohsen Kadivar, interview in the Iranian newspaper *Asr-e Ma*, on February 10, 1999, quoted in Radio Free Europe/Radio Liberty's *Iran Report* 2, no. 18, May 3, 1999. Kadivar, who has also advocated the clergy's retreat from the active sphere of governance in general, was arrested in February 1999, tried, and sentenced to 18 months in prison on the charges of "dissemination of lies and disturbing public opinion." See "Iran: Islam's Balancing Act," *Economist*, April 17, 1999, 48.

to speak out against the regime.[136] With their successive deaths in 1993 and 1994, however, pressure mounted to attempt to restore the unanimity between theological and political authority in the Islamic Republic by naming Khamenei as marja-ye taqlid. The effort was led by Muhammad Yazdi, then Iran's chief justice, and Majlis Speaker Nateq Nuri, and reaffirmed by a hasty campaign in the official press, which stressed the role of two political organizations in nominating Khamenei for this honor and highlighted the priority of political considerations in identifying candidates for marja'iyat.[137] The controversy drew in the parliament. In a telling demonstration of both the waning power of the leadership to command absolute obedience and the subversion of the religious hierarchy by purely political issues, only 155 of the 270 Majlis deputies signed the petition in support of Khamenei's bid to become the marja-ye taqlid, and 113 actually championed a competing effort to promote dissident Montazeri to this role.

Khamenei was eventually forced to publicly disavow the effort and withdraw himself, noting somewhat wryly that "the people are the most uncompromising on the subject of the marja'iyat."[138] He did, however, assert himself as the marja-ye taqlid for the Shia living outside of Iran, on the basis of a lack of senior religious models among Iran's coreligionists in countries such as Bahrain, Saudi Arabia, Kuwait, Iraq, and Lebanon, but even this presumption was dismissively rejected in Lebanon and elsewhere.[139] His bid to assume the highest post in the religious hierarchy

---

136. Grand Ayatollah Abu al-Qasim al-Musavi Al-Khoi was generally acknowledged as the most senior Shia cleric—even higher than Khomeini—until his death in 1992. Khoi was profoundly apolitical and after his death the regime in Tehran sought to promote successors who neither rival Khamenei nor create political uncertainties for the regime. Ayatollah Mohammad Reza Golpayegani had helped found the Qom seminary system and had voiced objections to the devolution of Islamic law under velayet-e faqih, but was 92 by the time he was acknowledged as a marja-ye taqlid and thus posed little threat. Ayatollah Mohammad Ali Araki possessed somewhat lesser religious credentials and a less influential circle of proponents, and he was considered something of a puppet candidate for marja-ye taqlid. See Barbara Allen Roberson, "Iran and the Shia Leadership," *The Gulf States Newsletter* 20, no. 506 (March 1995).

137. Those organizations were the Qom Society of Seminary Teachers and the Society of Combatant Clerics of Tehran (*Jame-ye Ruhanyiat-e Mobarez* or JRM). Ayatollah Ahmad Jannati voiced the prevailing opinion among Khamenei's backers that the traditional requirements for the marja'iyat are insufficient, and that political awareness and the ability to defend Islam as taught by Khomeini should hold the highest priority for selection of a new marja. Yazdi argued similarly that the marja must have "political and social consciousness so as to manage the Islamic community and society" and that the Islamic community had a compelling interest in limiting the marja'iyat to a single individual. See Gieling, "The *Marja'iya* in Iran," 779–80.

138. Khamenei speech, broadcast by the Voice of the Islamic Republic of Iran, December 14, 1994.

139. Augustus Richard Norton, *Hizballah of Lebanon: Extremist Ideals vs. Mundane Politics* (New York: Council on Foreign Relations, 1999), 21, 34. According to Norton, Sheikh Mohammad Husayn Fadlallah, "arguably the most influential Shi'i cleric in Lebanon" as the spiritual leader of Hezbollah, instead backed the candidacy of Grand Ayatollah Ali Mohammad Sistani, an Iranian cleric in Najaf.

withered without seriously damaging his mandate as the highest authority in the political hierarchy. However, the episode further fractured political unity among the clerical elite within Iran[140] and in the rest of the Shia world and completed the progressive marginalization of the traditional institutions of clerical authority. "By politicizing religious authority, the independent *mojtahed* will be marginalized and left without any significant importance and influence. The process of politicizing religious authority will reduce the independence of the clerical establishment, and its political and social activities and functions will be linked to political power games."[141]

---

140. The effort to promote Khamenei earned the scorn of several clerics who had remained largely loyal to the Islamic Republic, including Ayatollah Ahmad Azari-Qomi, as well as those already alienated from the government, such as Montazeri.

141. Mehdi Khalaji, *The Last Marja: Sistani and the End of Traditional Religious Authority in Shiism*, (Washington Institute for Near East Policy, Policy Focus no. 59, September 2006), 35, www.washingtoninstitute.org/pubPDFs/PolicyFocus59final.pdf (accessed April 17, 2008).

3

Agents of Change within Iran

The most powerful force of change within Iran may well be the very factor that goes unnoticed by either analysts or activists until some as yet unknown critical juncture makes it suddenly relevant. Recent developments across the region certainly suggest, if not the "global wave of democracy" promised by President Bush, then at the very least the prospect for the actions of hard-line autocrats occasionally to have the unintended consequence of facilitating democratic development. The Lebanese case, for example, in which the February 2005 assassination of former prime minister Rafiq Hariri sparked massive demonstrations that helped force Syria to withdraw its army after a thirty-year occupation, testifies to the galvanizing impact of an unforeseen tragedy. In Egypt, the combined pressure of the Bush administration and a newly robust civil society helped wrest modest concessions for a more free and fair electoral process from long-time President Hosni Mubarak. However, developments since 2005 in each of these cases also speak to the limitations on both international pressure and mass political action to produce genuinely dramatic transformations, particularly where the political culture is contested and international opprobrium is constrained.

Those outside Iran have not proved particularly prescient in forecasting that country's future; most of the abrupt changes that Iran has undergone over the past three decades—including the catalytic elections—have defied the expectations and predictions of both scholars and pundits. As a result, it is worthwhile to bear in mind that one likely path for Iran will be that which belies all predictions.

Youth and Students

The most obvious potential agent of change within Iran emanates from its own population and the postrevolutionary demographics that make this a disproportionately young society. In the aftermath of the Islamic Revolution, Iran's leaders adopted explicitly pronatalist policies, lauding large families and closing family planning clinics. The implications of those policies soon became clear; by the mid-1980s, Iran's birthrate was one of the highest in the world (3.9 percent), and the 1986 census revealed that Iran's population had mushroomed to fifty million.[1] Although Iran's leadership greeted

---

1. Jahangir Amuzegar, *Iran's Economy Under the Islamic Republic* (London: I.B. Tauris, 1993), 61–62.

these figures with evident pride—Prime Minister Mir Husayn Musavi described the milestone as one of the "major developments" in the Islamic world[2]—they recognized that the burden on public institutions and resources would quickly surpass the state's ability to meet it. That recognition generated one of the rare reversals of Iran's Islamic leadership on an issue of some ideological sensitivity. Over the period of a few years, the Islamic Republic adopted an effective and wide-ranging family-planning program that has received plaudits from the United Nations Population Fund.

Today, two-thirds of Iranians are under the age of thirty—too young to harbor meaningful memories of the prerevolutionary era—and 40 percent are under the age of eighteen.[3] Young Iranians tend to be well educated; primary school enrollment for both girls and boys is nearly universal, as is literacy.[4] Their childhoods were imprinted by the "consumer frenzy" that characterized the postwar reconstruction[5] and their lives are far more urbanized and mobile than those of their predecessors. Through their omnipresent (though still officially illegal) satellite dishes and burgeoning connections to the Internet, younger Iranians are intensely interconnected with the world beyond the Islamic Republic.

Not surprisingly, they are correspondingly frustrated. Pressures on Iran's young people are severe. Beyond the Islamic dress code for women, a wide range of religiously inspired strictures on Iran's political, social, and cultural life molds the experiences and options available to young Iranians. Overlaid with state enforcement of a strict interpretation of Islamic doctrine on issues such as alcohol and interactions with the opposite sex, the revolution inculcated Khomeini's austere and abstemious lifestyle as an ideal, which meant in practice that art, culture, and entertainment were severely proscribed during the early years of the Islamic Republic.

The omnipresence of religious strictures also appears to have redefined young Iranians' relationship with organized religion. A report prepared by the Tehran city council in 2000 estimated that "75 percent of the country's sixty million inhabitants and 86 percent of young students do not say their daily prayers."[6] While many continue to participate in religious ceremonies and commemorations, some do so simply because these events provide the

2.   Hassan Hakimian, "Population Dynamics in Post-Revolutionary Iran," in *The Economy of Iran: The Dilemmas of an Islamic State*, ed. Parvin Alizadeh (London: I.B. Tauris, 2000), 202.

3.   UNICEF, "At a Glance: Iran (Islamic Republic of)," www.unicef.org/infobycountry/iran_statistics.html#47 (accessed April 17, 2008).

4.   World Bank, "World Development Indicators," http://devdata.worldbank.org/wdi2005/Section2.htm (accessed April 17, 2008).

5.   Robin Wright, *The Last Great Revolution: Turmoil and Transformation in Iran* (New York: Alfred A. Knopf, 2000), 276.

6.   "Drugs and Prostitution Rampant among Youth: Government Report," Agence France-Presse, July 5, 2000.

few officially sanctioned opportunities for mixing with strangers of the opposite sex.[7]

There has been considerable liberalization since the early days of the revolution, particularly during the reformist heyday, as evidenced by the colorful and ever-shrinking headscarves and manteaus that adorn many urban women, the proliferation of coffeehouses and pop concerts in major cities, and the prevalence of dating rituals, as well as a host of more decadent activities. Still, social restrictions and the efforts required to evade their often arbitrary enforcement continue to chafe. As one young woman told a *Washington Post* reporter after morality police broke up a party she was attending, "I am so sick and tired of this meddling in our personal lives."[8]

In fact, the partial relaxation of social mores and restrictions may actually exacerbate the dissatisfaction of Iran's youth. As Abbas Kiarostami, one of Iran's most celebrated film producers, lamented, "We live in two worlds, internal and external, which do not fit together; this is a schizophrenic situation whose effects I dread, especially the effects on the young. I did not want [satellite] television to be showing my son without a break things that he cannot have."[9] And to whatever extent the reformist leadership alleviated some of the frustrations of the younger generation, the Ahmadinejad era has turned the clock back in many respects, including reimposition of more strenuous enforcement of Iran's dress code and even closing down a number of legendary traditional teahouses because they offered tobacco water pipes to their patrons.[10]

There are of course other pressures weighing on Iran's youth, predominantly economic ones (an issue that is covered in greater detail below) as well as the limitations of an overtaxed educational system. When it comes to jobs and education, Iran's young people are competing in an ever-wider pool for scarce resources. Despite significant expansion in the university system, there are places for only 400,000 of 1.5 million aspiring applicants—only half of those in state-subsidized universities—a reality that has made the historically challenging *concours* (national entrance exam) into an intense make-or-break qualification.[11]

As for jobs, "It doesn't really matter what your graduation grade is," one recent graduate told a reporter in June 2005. "It makes no difference what

---

7. Roxanne Varzi, *Warring Souls: Youth, Media, and Martyrdom in Post-Revolution Iran* (Durham, NC: Duke University Press, 2006), 122, 203.

8. Afshin Molavi, "Iran's Young Are Restless Under Islam," *Washington Post*, December 28, 1999.

9. Fariba Adelkhah, *Being Modern in Iran,* trans. Jonathan Derrick (New York: Columbia University Press, 2000), 172.

10. "Iran Snuffs Out Teahouses over Hubble-Bubbles," Fars News Agency, November 5, 2007, http://english.farsnews.com/newstext.php?nn=8608140335 (accessed April 17, 2008).

11. Adelkhah, *Being Modern in Iran,* 148.

contacts you have. You just cannot find a decent job."[12] Iran's economic distortions leave little reason for young Iranians to look toward their futures with optimism; the prospects of securing a job that provides a salary sufficient to support a family are extremely limited. In 1998, the average monthly salary for public sector employees—a significant component of the workforce given the dominant state role in the economy—was 48,000 tomans (approximately $100 at then exchange rates), whereas average monthly spending for a family of four was estimated at more than twice that amount.[13]

Even for those who can find a job, such salary levels put the trappings of independence and adulthood—in particular, marriage and an apartment—off-limits for all but the wealthy and the very upper middle class. The proportion of men between the ages of twenty and twenty-nine who live with their parents has mushroomed from 50 percent in 1984 to 75 percent in 2005, with corresponding increases for women as well.[14] As a study of Iranian youth by two noted economists concluded, "Together the schools and the formal labor market form a system of exclusion that leaves out the vast majority of educated youth."[15]

The construction of the gargantuan Imam Khomeini Grand Mosque in central Tehran provoked a telling response from one young software engineer in mid-2001. "We would have preferred to have had the biggest library in the world or the biggest computer center. There is no honor in having a mosque four hundred years from now. We would have preferred having a company like Microsoft here."[16]

The potential significance of the region's demographics has not been lost on politicians at home or abroad. Khatami actively courted the youth constituency and allied himself with student organizations until they eventually spurned his quietist approach. Notably, Rafsanjani explicitly geared his 2005 presidential campaign to appeal to the young, announcing that "Young people are our assets . . . we cannot expect their high performance while limiting their freedoms."[17] His campaign offices played banned pop music and deployed fashionable young women on roller skates wearing headbands with the candidate's name emblazoned in English. Nor is the power of Iran's young population lost on Iran's traditionalists. For hard-liners, Iran's restive youths traditionally were depicted as the revolution's Achilles' heel and a

---

12. "Iranian Brain Drain Looks Likely to Continue," Agence France-Presse, June 1, 2005.

13. Behzad Yaghmaian, *Social Change in Iran: An Eyewitness Account of Dissent, Defiance, and New Movements for Rights* (Albany: State University of New York Press, 2002), 23.

14. Djavad Salehi-Isfahani and David Egel, "Youth Exclusion in Iran: The State of Education, Employment and Family Formation" (Brookings Institution, Middle East Youth Initiative Working Paper no. 3, September 2007), 33.

15. Ibid., 37.

16. Matthew McAllester, "A Statement in Iran: Tehran's Grand Mosque a Symbol of Prayer, Pride—and Waste," *Newsday*, April 25, 2001.

17. "Rafsanjani Launches Reformist Campaign Plan," Reuters, June 1, 2005.

potent vehicle for external subversion. "An onslaught, aiming to pervert the youth's morals and beliefs, has started from abroad, which is supported from within," Ayatollah Nasser Makarem Shirazi said in 2001. "Destroying the youth's morals and beliefs is to betray the country and its independence."[18]

Ever the savvy balancer of power and ideology, Ayatollah Khamenei has adopted a more nuanced stance. In 2001, he described Iran's millions of yearning young people as "a tumultuous river that is full of riches," which carried with it the potential to develop or devastate the country.

> This river can be approached in two ways. One is that you adopt a scientific and intelligent approach and then, first, recognize the importance of this river, and second identify the areas which need the water of this river. Then you should formulate plans, build the necessary canals, and direct the water to the areas which need it. . . . In this way, this phenomenon will be turned into a unique and exceptional point of strength, for which the people of Iran can never thank the Almighty enough. . . . The other approach is to abandon this dynamic and tumultuous river on its own, and fail to carry out any thinking and planning about it. The result is that the farms will run dry and the orchards will be destroyed. In addition, the water of this river will be completely wasted. At best, it will just flow into a reservoir of salty water and will go to waste. The other possibility is that it will flow into swamps here and there, where various forms of germs and pests congregate. The worst case scenario is when these waters change into floods, which is going to destroy all the achievements of the nation. Without careful planning and hard work, this is going to be the outcome.[19]

Even as the reformist period crashed to a halt, youth remain a salient political constituency—critical to securing sufficient votes to retain control of Iran's elective institutions and to assuring social calm for an insecure regime. As a result, conservatives have also made conspicuous efforts to court the young, even as they have helped roll back some of the liberalization measures of the Khatami period. In September 2004, Rahim Safavi, then commander of the Revolutionary Guards, dismissed criticism of Iranian students who sport Western clothes or hairstyles. "You see, we must admit that in terms of taste, there are differences," Safavi acknowledged. "In fact, this is natural everywhere in the world and is not specific to Iran. The world is changing, and we must not expect our children to be like us. . . . But my personal analysis is

---

18. "Top Cleric Warns of Foreign Onslaught to 'Pervert' Iran Youth," Islamic Republic News Agency, July 20, 2001.

19. Khamenei speech, delivered on a visit to Gilan province, May 2, 2001, broadcast on Vision of the Islamic Republic of Iran Network 1 at 1713 GMT on May 4, 2001.

that the typical attitude of our young people in this country is very positive and acceptable."[20]

Compared with the ebullience of the reformist outreach to young Iranians, Ahmadinejad has adopted a more paternalistic approach, focused on cultivating ideological orthodoxy among young Iranians while also funneling more financial resources their way by mandating bank loans directed to young people. "With the right tools, we can define what is happiness for the youth," Mehrdad Bazrpash, the president's twenty-something youth advisor told an American reporter in 2005. "It's the job of the state to create and transfer this culture of sacrifice to these youngsters."[21] Most of his administration's efforts appeared designed to reinforce Iran's revolutionary zeal, such as constructing mausoleums for war martyrs on university campuses. Less frequently, Ahmadinejad appeared to court more liberalized youth, such as his push in April 2006 to permit women into soccer stadiums to attend matches. In 2007, Ahmadinejad backed efforts to lower the voting age to fifteen, in direct conflict with the conservative parliament, which had only recently raised it to eighteen.

At the same time as he sought to extend the regime's popular base through populist programs and new initiatives to reinforce cultural orthodoxy, Ahmadinejad helped exacerbate the alienation and resentment that pervade youth opinion in Iran. Censorship of books and other media has intensified dramatically; Islamic dress codes and other social prohibitions are being enforced with renewed vigor.

Historically, student activism has proved to be a critical component of successful political mobilization in Iran, as well as in other developing countries. In the lead-up to the 1979 revolution, students played a critical role in expressing dissatisfaction with the monarchy and developing linkages between the clergy and traditionally secular constituencies; in the aftermath, the student seizure of the American Embassy helped consolidate the power of the radical Islamist elements of the postrevolutionary regime while marginalizing moderates.

Moreover, since the revolution, the student population has expanded at rates higher than that of the general population, as higher educational opportunities have opened up to segments of the population who previously had little access. In 1979, 140,000 Iranians were enrolled in universities; in 2003, that number was 1.15 million. A variety of factors—including the brain drain problem, the postrevolutionary cultural purges within Iran's university system, and affirmative action policies for ideologically favored elements

---

20. Hoseyn Zakariaei, "Special Interview with General Doctor Seyyed Yahya Safavi," *Jomhuri-ye Islami*, September 21, 2004, www.jeslami.com/1383/13830631/13830631_jomhori_islami_10_jebheh_va_jang.HTML#matlab_1 (accessed May 9, 2008).

21. Scott Peterson, "Iranian Leader Eyes Key Constituency: Young People," *Christian Science Monitor*, October 28, 2005.

of the Iranian population—have also had the effect of diversifying Iran's student population by class and geographic background.[22]

Iran's primary student group is known as Daftar-e Takhim-e Vahdat, or the Office for the Consolidation of Unity. The organization was founded during the heady early days of the revolution and, as its name implies, shortly thereafter absorbed by the regime itself as a means of channeling student activism and inculcating official Islamist ideology. Over time, however, Daftar and a spin-off student organization, Ettahadieh-e Anjomanha-ye Eslami (the Union of Islamic Associations) evolved into distinctly autonomous and politicized vehicles for the expression of student interests. Daftar experienced a heyday in the early years of Khatami's first term, when it served as "a paramount force exposing the judiciary, the security forces, and other state institutions controlled by conservatives."[23] At the same time, however, the newly empowered student movement became the focus of critical scrutiny by conservatives and the "pressure groups" of hard-line thugs allied with them.

Iran's student organizations followed an evolutionary path that mirrored the larger changes in society. During Rafsanjani's second term as president, Iranian officials endeavored to temper the fiery young radicals who led its student organizations, banning Daftar from holding a separate anti-American rally to mark the November 4 anniversary of the seizure of the U.S. Embassy.[24] Five years later, in 1998, Daftar defied the line and shunned the traditional theatrics on the very same anniversary. Instead, the student group organized a march to the former embassy compound and listened as Ibrahim Asgharzadeh, one of the chief organizers of the seizure who reemerged under Khatami as a radically liberal Tehran city councilor, invited the former hostages to return for a visit as guests of the Islamic Republic. "Regarding relations with America," Asgharzadeh told the assembled crowd of twenty-five hundred, "we must look to the future and not to the past."[25] The event was as close to an apology for that regrettable episode as any official Iranian institution or individual has ever come, and an example of the entrepreneurial audacity that characterized the student movement during the early years of the Khatami era.

Only two years after Khatami's first inauguration, however, the rising frustration of the student movement with the slow pace of reforms and the persistent repression by conservatives led to the first, and most serious, explosion of the reformist period. It was triggered by two provocations that occurred on July 7, 1999—the closure of *Salaam*, one of the pioneers

22. "Student Movement: The Harbinger of a New Era in Iran," International Institute for the Study of Islam in the Modern World newsletter, no. 4, 1999.

23. Yaghmaian, *Social Change in Iran*, 2002, 81.

24. Mehdi Moslem, *Factional Politics in Post-Khomeini Iran* (Syracuse, NY: Syracuse University Press, 2002), 226.

25. "Iran Islamic Students Offer Olive Branch to U.S.," Reuters, November 2, 1998.

crusading liberal journalism in post-Khomeini Iran, and the passage by the right-wing parliament of a restrictive new press law that would curb the blossoming media and subject journalists to more severe penalties for transgressing Iran's cultural or political "redlines." The protests initially consisted of only a relatively small gathering of Tehran University students, but after that demonstration was viciously subdued by the security forces and right-wing thugs, the situation changed dramatically.

The violence intensified popular outrage and boosted participation in the demonstrations to crowds of more than ten thousand. Meanwhile, demonstrations to express solidarity with the students of Tehran were organized in eighteen other major Iranian cities. The focus of the demonstrators began to widen, as slogans decrying the new press law soon gave way to demands for wholesale political changes to the Islamic system. Students were seen defacing official symbols and portraits of the supreme leader. The international media speculated that the protests were the start of a new revolution, while "Iranian exiles . . . began to dream about returning and re-creating a homeland where sales of French wine would outnumber chadors."[26] It was the most serious unrest that the Islamic Republic had experienced in more than two decades, and it shook all elements of Iran's political elite—as well as many segments of the population—to its core, not least because it began in the heart of the capital city.

Ultimately, of course, the outcome of the July 1999 student activism represents a seminal disappointment in Iran's evolution, and a turning point for the fates of the reform movement as well as the student leadership. The protests devolved into violence, as hard-line "pressure groups" took matters into their own hands; rather than join the action, most of Tehran's twelve million residents tried, uneasily, to go about their business as usual. And from Khatami on down, the reformists in government for the most part failed to come to the defense of the students and sanctioned the decision by the security forces to break up the protests. Several days later, Iranian newspapers published the text of a letter from senior Revolutionary Guard commanders to Khatami, in which they threatened to seize power if he did not subdue the unrest. At the time, Khatami reportedly considered resigning to pave the way for new presidential elections.[27]

In the end, the episode embittered both the students, who were justifiably disillusioned by their abandonment by the reformists in power, and their patrons in government, some of whom felt that their "stealth" effort to quietly engineer significant political change was undermined by the impetuous actions of the students. In that sense, the July 1999 protests were a turning

26. Geneive Abdo and Jonathan Lyons, *Answering Only to God: Faith and Freedom in Twenty-First Century Iran* (New York: Henry Holt, 2003), 197.

27. Buchta, *Who Rules Iran?*, 190.

point for the student movement and, more broadly, for the fate of the reformist enterprise. For their part, the hard-liners took heart in the ambivalence of
public sentiment and the ease with which they were able to repel even the
most serious challenge to the norms and institutions of the Islamic Republic. That success inevitably came with a long-term price; as noted intellectual
Sadeq Zibakalam acknowledged, "When the police beats a first- or second-
year student on the head with a truncheon today, the action will cost the
system dearly in the long term."[28]

The July 1999 unrest also laid the seeds for the official disempowerment of
the student movement, as well as for the emergence of paralyzing divisions
in strategic vision among the student leaders themselves. The conservative
crackdown began to take its toll, with key leaders behind bars and reportedly subject to torture and other inhumane treatment. "Our language used
to be more courageous," Majid Haji Babaei, a leader of Daftar, conceded in
late 2004. "But we were beaten up and even thrown out of windows; we were
suppressed, and many went to jail. Naturally, some students felt disappoint-
ed, and the risk of political involvement also got higher."[29]

In the aftermath of the July 1999 unrest, Daftar struggled with internal
contention among its leadership over strategy and focus—contention that
became so fierce that it sparked brawls.[30] By late 2000, a number of influential student leaders had come to the recognition that meaningful reform
would not be possible without explicitly changing the governing system, and
advocated embarking on a campaign of civil disobedience. Others balked
at "bypassing Khatami" and rejecting the Islamic Republic in total, and because neither group was prepared to disavow the other publicly, the student
organizations languished.

Student activism remains episodically powerful, as in the November
2002 demonstrations protesting the death sentence issued in the case of
Hashem Aghajari, a university professor and Iraq war veteran who was
convicted on charges of apostasy. Aghajari's purported crime stemmed
from a speech in which he questioned the clerical monopoly on interpreting Islam, suggesting that individuals need not follow clerical mandates
blindly and further arguing that Islam should be reinterpreted by each
generation to fit the exigencies of the time. The rallies generated considerable domestic and international attention and helped lead to the eventual
reconsideration of Aghajari's sentence.

---

28. "Sadeq Zibakalam: 'Dormant Universities and Students Will Not Serve the Interests of
    the System,'" *Azad*, June 25, 2002.
29. Megan K. Stack, "In Clerics' Iran, Children of the Revolution Seek Escape," *Los Angeles
    Times*, December 26, 2004.
30. Mohammad Ravaqi, "The Story of the Friends Who Became Enemies," *Seda-ye Edalat*,
    May 28, 2002.

Again in June 2003, thousands of students massed in the streets of Tehran for several nights of increasingly forceful protests. Although the demonstrations were initially sparked by reports of the privatization of some state universities, they quickly escalated to vocalize vehemently antiregime rhetoric such as "Death to Khamenei!" In a final break with their former icon, they also demanded the resignation of President Khatami.[31] It is worth noting that in this case as in prior ones, student activism was initially sparked not by grand political grievances, but by the more mundane pressures of school fees and cafeteria food.[32] Once begun, however, these demonstrations exhibited a deepening outrage among young Iranians, who brandished photos of imprisoned activists and placed large swaths of tape over their mouths as a stark commentary about the state of free speech in the Islamic Republic.

The Ahmadinejad administration took a preemptive approach to student politics. The president, a veteran of the revolutionary student movement who regularly describes himself as a simple professor, signaled his intentions toward academia by appointing a cleric to head Tehran University, the nation's flagship campus. Faculty members involved with reformist politics found themselves facing early retirement; some student leaders were expelled or imprisoned, while others were released and effectively encouraged to emigrate. Ahmadinejad has publicly inveighed against "liberal and secular university lectures" and pledged to change the political environment on campuses across the country.[33]

As a result, student activism since 2005 has been restricted to a handful of small but memorable encounters, such as an episode in December 2006 when several students interrupted an Ahmadinejad speech at Amir Kabir University marking the annual Students' Day to burn the president's picture, shouting "Death to the Dictator." Similar incidents took place at Tehran University in May, October, and again in December 2007, during the commemoration of Students' Day at a number of major urban universities. At each demonstration, turnout was modest but the message was defiant in its opposition to the president's approach to governance.

Student mobilization has special significance in Iran, given the history of the revolution. Following a crackdown that took place in early 2001, the Tehran office of Daftar issued a pointed warning, referencing one of the seminal figures of the Islamic Revolution to underscore their frustration. "Some years ago, addressing Mohammad Reza Pahlavi, the late Engineer [Mehdi] Bazargan

---

31. Ali Akbar Dareini, "Clashes in Iran Intensify," Associated Press, June 12, 2003.

32. Karl Vick, "Protests Grow for Iranian Professor: Thousands of Students Challenge Conservatives," *Washington Post*, November 13, 2002. The November 2002 rallies protesting the death sentence handed down to academic Hashem Aghajari were reported to have escalated out of a spontaneous student outburst over the quality of cafeteria food.

33. "Iran's Ahmadinejad Calls for Purge of Liberal University Teachers," Associated Press, September 5, 2006.

said: We are the last generation that will speak to you in this language," the statement read. "We remind those who are in charge of determining the interests of the nation that reforms are the final way of remedying the rupture of the generations. If the monopolists stop reforms with all-around pressures and illegal actions, it is clear in advance, let such not be."[34] Five years later, another student leader echoed that theme in condemning the crackdown on university politics under Ahmadinejad. "They have sent our professors into early retirement; prevented many students from continuing their studies; forbidden not only protest, but even the act of breathing freely; and transformed our universities into military garrisons," Armin Salmasi said. "Don't think that our patience is unlimited. Someday, the pot will boil over."[35]

Ultimately, though, it is not clear that youth dissatisfaction can or will prove the critical factor that topples or significantly redirects the Islamic Republic. The presumption, particularly from outside Iran, is that frustration among Iran's young, well-educated population will eventually force a reckoning inside Iran, a presumption cultivated by the courageous acts of the student movement and the adventurousness and defiance with which many Iranians treat the regime's social taboos. "Being free from memories of the violent crackdowns of the early postrevolution years, the youth were now equally free from fear," writes Kaveh Basmenji in his study on Iran's youth culture.[36] However, Basmenji notes that this lack of fear has not produced the anticipated embrace of revolution: "Excited radio and television broadcasts from Los Angeles frequently call on the youngsters to finish the regime in one decisive mass movement. However, the youth seem to react as indifferently towards such calls as they react to calls by the state media to take part in rallies against the United States and Israel."[37]

Rather than protest, a not inconsiderable proportion of young Iranians have rebelled against the strictures of the Islamic state by dissociating from politics. One young Iranian explained to an American reporter in 2007 that the struggles of daily life, particularly those involved with managing the balance between public laws and private lives, distract the country's large youth cohort from focusing on the larger issues at stake in Iran today. "They make you obsessed with these little things, so that you don't think about the big issues."[38]

---

34. "Statement of the Tehran Council of the Unity Consolidation Movement Regarding the New Cycle of the Judicial System's Conflict with the Reformers and the Students," Iranian Students' News Agency, February 28, 2001.

35. Bahman Nirumand, "Ahmadinejad's Cultural Revolution," Qantara.de Dialogues with the Islamic World, www.qantara.de/webcom/show_article.php/_c-476/_nr-693/i.html (accessed April 17, 2008).

36. Kaveh Basmenji, *Tehran Blues: Youth Culture in Iran* (London: Saqi Books, 2005), 25–26.

37. Ibid., 26.

38. Anne Barnard, "Iran's Young and Restless," *Boston Globe*, February 3, 2007, www.boston.com/news/world/blog/2007/02/irans_young_and_1.html (accessed April 17, 2008).

Instead of dissent or agitation, some young Iranians find other ways to express their dissatisfaction with their circumstances—by leaving the country or by losing themselves in drugs. Ahmadinejad's economic and social policies have only exacerbated the exodus of Iran's educated classes that began in dramatic fashion with the revolution. The brain drain is a direct function of the dearth of economic opportunities and the political frustration that was intensified under the factional infighting of the Khatami period. Young Iranians joke with some bitterness that an Iranian PhD qualifies its holder for a pizza delivery job overseas.[39] A 2005 government poll of sixteen thousand young people throughout Iran found that 44 percent would leave the country if they could.[40]

Statistics are inevitably hazy, but estimates suggest that between 150,000 and 200,000 Iranians leave the country by legal or illegal means each year. The IMF has characterized Iran's brain drain as one of the highest in the world.[41] Iranian economist Fariborz Raisdana describes the brain drain as "a utilitarian approach," explaining, "We cannot offer them opportunities in the fields of politics, economics, or science. So they simply move on."[42] In 2002, the government allocated 100 billion rials ($12.5 million) to combat this problem.[43] Requests for visas to Europe and the United States reportedly multiplied in the aftermath of Ahmadinejad's election.

For those who cannot leave, drugs are an all too ready alternative, thanks to Iran's 936-km shared border with Afghanistan, which has long been the world's leading producer of opium. The government itself has acknowledged the degeneration of Iranian youth in an official report describing the prevalence of drug use and estimating that prostitution had risen by 635 percent among Iranian high school students.[44] Although statistics on substance abuse in Iran are subject to some debate, most official Iranian and UN studies suggest the country has somewhere in the range of two million addicts. UNICEF describes Iran as having one of the highest rates of drug usage in the region.[45] Although opium has a long history in the region, a former Tehran municipal

39. "Iranian Brain Drain Looks Likely to Continue," Agence France-Presse, June 1, 2005.

40. Barbara Slavin, "New Attitudes Color Iranian Society, Culture," *USA Today*, March 1, 2005.

41. William J. Carrington and Enrica Detragiache, "How Extensive Is the Brain Drain?" *Finance & Development* 36, no. 2 (June 1999); Afshin Molavi, "Iranian Youths Seeking to Escape," *Washington Post*, September 7, 2003.

42. "Iranian Brain Drain Looks Likely to Continue," Agence France-Presse, June 1, 2005.

43. "Young Iranians Flock out of the Country to Live Abroad," Agence France-Presse, May 17, 2002.

44. "Drugs and Prostitution Rampant among Youth: Government Report," Agence France-Presse, July 5, 2000.

45. John Calabrese, "Iran's War on Drugs: Holding the Line?" Middle East Institute Policy Brief no. 3, December 2007, 6, www.mideasti.org/files/irans-war-on-drugs.pdf (accessed April 17, 2008); UNICEF, "At a Glance: Iran (Islamic Republic of)," www.unicef.org/infoby-country/iran.html (accessed April 17, 2008).

official noted that "the pattern of the drug abuse has changed, and most of the addicts are young."[46] Alongside drugs come other forms of social pathology and dislocation, including the skyrocketing rates of HIV, prostitution, divorce, and suicide that Iran experiences.

Another segment of young Iran—particularly those with the means to do so—copes with the country's social and economic constraints by turning inward. This has distanced today's young Iranians from their predecessors, many of whom dove headlong into the 1979 revolution and helped build the Islamic Republic. "When I was a youth, we were revolutionaries, and we were ready to pay the price," commented Hamid Reza Jalaipour, a sociologist and onetime student activist who ran a string of reformist newspapers that were closed for violating regime taboos. "These days the youth are not ready to pay. They prefer to depoliticize, and the conservatives are very happy about that. They are looking for passive masses."[47]

Depoliticization of youth has helped fuel a boom in Western-style pop psychology or *khod-sazi*, described by scholar Roxanne Varzi as "one of the most important components of young, urban Iranian life in the form of hypnosis classes, yoga, self-help books, Jungian study circles, and Sufi poetry reading circles, among other things."[48] Still other young Iranians simply seek socialization and enjoyment where they can find it—participating in the robust underground party scene, cruising public parks in Iran's elaborately choreographed dating scene, or using family and religious gatherings as a mechanism for pursuing a semi-independent social life.

This imperative was manifest in the national jubilation that transfixed Iran on November 6, 1997, when Iran's national soccer team qualified for the World Cup and its cities were engulfed in ecstatic and spontaneous revelry that featured every sort of un-Islamic behavior as well as clashes with right-wing thugs. These scenes were repeated after the June 1998 defeat of the U.S. team in the World Cup and during a June 2005 World Cup qualifying match, when female fans stormed the stadium demanding their right to attend the match. "They slice through traffic on their motorbikes, racing each other at breakneck speed while holding their mobile phones. They listen to heavy metal, read Günter Grass, and admire Tom Cruise. They don't go to the mosque the way their parents did, and they have given up on politics."[49]

Young Iranians are undoubtedly an agent of change, but how they will express this agitation continues to have many concerned, particularly given

---

46. Basmenji, *Tehran Blues*, 311.
47. Megan K. Stack, "In Clerics' Iran, Children of the Revolution Seek Escape," *Los Angeles Times*, December 26, 2004.
48. Varzi, *Warring Souls*, 10.
49. Dan De Luce, "Anger Grows among Children of Iran's 25-Year-Old Revolution," *Guardian* (Manchester), February 9, 2004.

the surprising outcome of the June 2005 presidential election. Ultimately, it is not yet clear whether they will press for specific rights and privileges from their government—in other words, greater political participation and economic opportunity—or if they can be satisfied with a simple diminution in the manifold pressures that they face. To some extent, it is clear that the reform movement presumed incorrectly that young Iranians cared more about esoteric political principles, such as a free press, than they did about their own lives and livelihoods. The fading fortunes of that movement suggest that progressive politics and a focus on expanding civil rights and freedoms may be the prerogative of the privileged.

In addition, both the legacy of the revolution and the ascendance of Ahmadinejad testify to the readiness of Iran's young *mostazafan* (dispossessed) to cede democracy for a darker outcome. A number of Ahmadinejad's key advisers are in their twenties, representative of a postrevolutionary generation whose frustration with the Islamic regime lies more with its latter-day relaxation and the enrichment of its senior figures than with any aspiration for a more democratic order. As this portrayal of young members of Iran's Basij militia suggests, the politics of the Muslim world show all too clearly how the resentments of youth can facilitate the rise of those who would embrace authoritarianism and a more rigorous interpretation of Islamic social codes.

> Their sleeves reach their wrists, their shoes are scuffed. . . . Many eke out a living by renting motorbikes to work as messengers or bike taxis; hordes of them idle sullenly on their bikes near Tehran's grand bazaar. With that sort of work, it will take them an epoch to raise enough money to get married. The Basij might give them a small stipend and help cover holidays at the Caspian Sea, but it cannot buy them an apartment or sustain a life.[50]

Alternatively, Iran's frustrated young population may prove more willing to compromise than many expect. The past eight years evidences the utility of a modest social liberalization in staving off popular unrest. So long as there are some social outlets—parks, cafes, football matches—along with the means of evading or resisting restrictions and a black market to satisfy any taboo, young Iranians may suborn continuing political stagnation. As one youth magazine put it after the original 1997 soccer celebrations, "The presence of hundreds of thousands of people and the eruption of joy and happiness on the streets of Tehran was an unexpected and unusual event. To many young people freedom does not mean the freedom of

---

50. Azadeh Moaveni, "The Eminem Fan Who Polices Tehran's Morals," *Time*, July 29, 2005, www.time.com/time/world/article/0,8599,1088518,00.html (accessed April 17, 2008).

speech, the right to public gathering, the freedom of association, or the liberal or religious interpretation of freedom. To many youth, freedom means happiness. . . . Happiness is a need for humanity. Happiness is a need in our society today."[51]

Economy

One of the primary complaints of Iran's students and young people is the lack of economic opportunities and prospects available to them. This grievance is shared widely across society. Indeed, as the 2005 presidential elections once again demonstrated, the shape and strength of the Iranian economy represents one of the most critical variables for determining the country's future course. When the price of oil sank below $20 a barrel, Iran's president championed a "dialogue of civilizations"; as the price veered past $60, his successor appealed for Iran's longtime nemesis Israel to be "wiped from the map." Iran's ambitions and its capacity to undertake them are shaped in large part by the state's balance sheet, as is the international community's response.

The salience of the economy for Iran's future development and influence has been heightened by the postrevolutionary government's problematic management of the economy and the growing centrality of economic well-being to the regime's legitimacy. Iran is a wealthy country that boasts a highly educated population, abundant natural resources, and a well-developed infrastructure. Since the revolution, however, the economy has experienced repeated and profound disruptions. The revolution, the war, the population explosion, and the oil price collapse of the 1980s together meant that Iran's income experienced a "breathtaking" decline during the Islamic Republic's first decade.[52] The country's population explosion during the same period meant that the ramifications of the economic deterioration was felt even more sharply on a per capita basis. Although postwar reconstruction and growth have boosted per capita income back to its prerevolutionary high, "the memory of the harsh times in the 1980s continues to haunt most Iranians" and exacerbates popular responses to the more recent economic uncertainties, particularly rising inflation, under Ahmadinejad.[53]

At the root of Iran's economic dilemmas are the Islamic Republic's policies, which have resulted in a large and inefficient state sector, a bloated bureaucracy, massive subsidies, and endemic corruption. Iran's resource base— approximately 10 percent of the world's proven oil reserves and the world's

---

51. *Omid-e Javan*, June 29, 1998, as quoted in Yaghmaian, *Social Change in Iran*, 2002, 53.
52. Djavad Salehi-Isfahani, "Revolution and Redistribution in Iran: Poverty and Inequality 25 Years Later," December 2007, forthcoming in the *Journal of Economic Inequality*, www.filebox.vt.edu/users/salehi/Iran_poverty_trend.pdf (accessed May 9, 2008), 6.
53. Ibid., 8.

second largest reserves of natural gas—has helped sustain the Islamic Republic; petroleum revenues provide two-thirds of government spending. However, even with respect to the country's lifeblood, Iranian policy has imposed costly constraints. As a result of constitutional restrictions prohibiting foreign ownership of Iranian oil through concessions or production-sharing agreements, Tehran devised a formula for international participation in its petroleum industry known as a "buy-back" agreement. Under this formula, international corporations receive payment for their costs and a prenegotiated profit. It has proven a profoundly inefficient way of developing Iran's most significant resource—the low rates of return and short time horizons have dampened interest in Iran's energy industry and resulted in lengthy and arduous negotiations between the National Iranian Oil Company and potential investors.

In addition to Iran's self-imposed constraints on developing its resources, a robust regime of U.S. economic sanctions has had a deterrent effect on Iran's ability to attract the massive infusions of international capital needed to modernize and expand its aging energy infrastructure and marketize its underutilized gas resources. The sanctions preclude any business activities by American companies or individuals, and while U.S. secondary sanctions on foreign companies have yet to be enforced by Washington, they have increased the costs of doing business in Iran. U.S. sanctions also place critical technology for liquefied natural gas off-limits to Iran, and the U.S. policy of promoting pipeline routes for Central Asian resources that bypass both Iran and Russia means that Iran may be increasingly disconnected from regional and international energy transportation routes.

Ahmadinejad's provocative rhetoric along with rising tensions between Tehran and Washington have also had a significant impact on Iran's energy sector through a combination of multilateral economic sanctions, new U.S. efforts to restrict Iranian access to the international financial system, declines in Iran's credit rating, and the voluntary departure of some Western banks and other firms from the Iranian market. These trends have meant a significant shift in patterns of foreign investment and trade with Iran away from some of its traditional trading partners in Europe. A number of European governments have actively dissuaded their companies from entering new deals in Iran, and while Chinese and Russian firms have aggressively taken advantage of new opportunities, it is not clear that they can provide the technology and expertise for the complicated work of reviving Iran's flagging oil production.

The lack of foreign investment means that Iran's oil production is declining steadily at an estimated rate of two hundred thousand barrels per day each year, producing 5 percent less than its OPEC quota in 2006. In addition, despite its mammoth gas reserves, Iran is actually a net importer of gas, largely because of its "glacial pace" in attracting investment and advancing new projects, and it now appears unlikely that Iran will produce sufficient quantities of natural gas to export for at least another decade.[54] Iranian officials have described the state of the country's oil sector as on the precipice of a fundamental crisis. Ahmadinejad's oil minister resigned in August 2007, telling the audience at his farewell ceremony that "if we do not find a solution to the energy problem in the next fifteen years, the country will face a catastrophe."[55]

Intertwined with the problems that plague the supply side of Iran's oil sector is the skyrocketing rate of internal consumption, a function of subsidies that keep gasoline prices at a mere eight hundred rials per liter (or approximately thirty-five cents per gallon.)[56] The artificially low prices have contributed to a culture of inefficiency in the use of gasoline, along with considerable waste and smuggling. As a result, oil-rich Iran is forced to import ever-increasing amounts of fuel each year, as much as 40 percent of the sixty-five million liters of gasoline consumed each day.[57] The average growth in energy consumption is increasing more quickly than the rate of population increase.[58] The conservative-dominated Majlis rejected any price increases, forcing the regime to raid its oil stabilization fund to pay for some of these imports.[59] This explicitly violates the original intent of the fund, which was to buffer the Iranian economy during periods of low oil prices and to amplify investment and job creation. The cost of gasoline imports—which totaled $17 billion over the past three years—has become such an obvious economic and strategic liability to Iran that in June 2007 the current government mandated an unpopular new rationing program.[60]

Beyond the gasoline subsidies, as much as 25 percent of Iran's gross domestic product each year goes toward preserving below-market prices for a range of staple consumer goods, such as bread. Economists persistently argue that redirecting the total cost of these and other subsidies on basic consumer goods would be more than sufficient to fund a generous social safety net for truly needy Iranians. However, raising gasoline prices to market levels would have a catastrophic impact on the average Iranian, boosting

---

54. Stanley Reed, "Surprise: Oil Woes in Iran," *Business Week*, November 30, 2006, www.businessweek.com/globalbiz/content/nov2006/gb20061130_396971.htm?chan=globalbiz_europe_more+of+today's+top+stories (accessed April 17, 2008); Simon Webb, "Iran Still a Decade Away from Major Gas Exports," Reuters, January 17, 2007.

55. Stuart Williams, "Sacked Iran Minister Warns of Oil 'Catastrophe'," Agence France-Presse, August 19, 2007.

56. "Iran Relieved of Fuel Import Concerns," *Iran Daily*, January 13, 2005, www.iran-daily.com/1383/2189/html/economy.htm (accessed April 17, 2008).

57. Ibid.

58. "Energy Consumption Up," *Iran Daily*, May 16, 2002.

59. "Forex Fund Withdrawals Legal," *Iran Daily*, January 13, 2005, www.iran-daily.com/1383/2189/html/economy.htm#37779 (accessed April 17, 2008).

60. "The Statement of the Islamic Iran Participation Front: Assessment of the Performance of Ahmadinejad's Government in the Field of Oil and Gas," *Etemad*, October 20, 2007, www.etemaad.com/Released/86-07-25/133.htm#49448 (accessed May 9, 2008).

the cost of transportation alone from an estimated eighty cents per person per day to more than ten dollars.[61] And unless skillfully managed, revamping the subsidies or undertaking any truly ambitious program of structural reforms would inevitably fuel inflation, which already sap Iranians living at the economic margins of their purchasing power, to double-digit levels.

Joblessness and underemployment are far more prevalent than are formally reported. A 1998 Ministry of Education solicitation to hire 500 custodians drew 150,000 applications, including 400 from individuals with bachelor's degrees.[62] Iranian newspaper articles suggest that over 70 percent of public employees are forced to take on a second job in order to meet the rising cost of living. Senior managers in state enterprises often take on multiple posts, in contravention of the labor law.[63] Educated professionals frequently supplement their incomes by operating their cars as taxicabs. As one observer trenchantly put it, "economic marginalization of the wage earners transformed Iran into a nation of cab drivers."[64] This phenomenon also contributes to the breakdown in the social fabric, as family life—traditionally the centerpiece of social activity—suffers as a result.

And despite the emphasis of the revolution's rhetoric on improving social justice, Iran remains a country of stark division between rich and poor, where 10 percent of the population controls 76 percent of the resources.[65] The government itself acknowledges that 12 percent of the population lives in absolute poverty, meaning they cannot provide for basic human needs such as food and shelter, according to the director general of the Antipoverty Program of the Ministry of Welfare and Social Security.[66] Ahmadinejad skillfully highlighted these class grievances in his 2005 campaign video, contrasting the luxurious residence of Gholamhussein Karbaschi, his popular but presumably shady predecessor as Tehran's mayor, with his own cramped quarters in a working-class neighborhood. Relative deprivation in an economy that has registered significant real growth in recent years may prove to be a more potent factor than pure hardship with respect to mobilizing the population against the system.[67]

---

61. "Waste, Trafficking Force Oil-rich Iran to Import Fuel," Agence France-Presse, November 25, 2002.

62. Yaghmaian, *Social Change in Iran*, 2002, 23.

63. "The 'Second Job' Phenomenon," *Iran Daily*, May 14, 2002.

64. Yaghmaian, *Social Change in Iran*, 2002, 157.

65. "High Revenues Give Ahmadinejad a Chance to Fulfill Pledge to Poor," Agence France-Presse, June 29, 2005.

66. "Official Provides Statistics on Poverty in Iran," July 26, 2005, *Siyasat-e Ruz*, July 21, 2005.

67. The International Monetary Fund reports that Iran has registered growth rates of more than 6 percent for the past two years, but also indicates that government spending has expanded to absorb the higher-than-budgeted oil revenues, fueling inflation and other economic distortions. See IMF, "Staff Report for the 2004 Article IV Consultation," August 20, 2004.

The manifold restrictions tend to force productive economic activity onto the black market. Indeed, the restrictions within Iran—combined with the U.S. embargo—have directed much of Iran's wealth into Dubai, helping to fuel the phenomenal rise of that city and leaving it inextricably intertwined with the internal Iranian economy.

Iran's economic problems have extraordinary political relevance because they are the consequence of human failure rather than actual indigence. Iran is a profoundly wealthy country, expected to earn a record $70 billion in oil revenues in 2008. But it suffers from a legacy of incoherent and inconsistent economic policymaking. Immediately after the Islamic Revolution, serious discord emerged among the political elite between those who have been dubbed "Islamic socialists," who advocated a larger state economic role to cultivate a more socially just order based on the radical theories of Mahmud Taleqani, Mohammad Baqer Sadr, and others, and those who, either out of institutional interest or a more conservative interpretation of Islamic law, prioritized the legal sanctity of private property and private enterprise. Consistent with traditional Shia jurisprudence, which generally holds the sanctity of private property to be inviolable, Ayatollah Khomeini was a reliably staunch defender of property rights and the role of the private sector.[68] This philosophical orientation was reinforced by the ulema's strong alliance with the bazaaris, Iran's traditional merchant community, whose financial support was crucial to the anti-Shah movement and the theocracy.[69]

In practice, however, tortuous political competition, chaos on the streets, sanctions and international financial pressures, and eventually the war with Iraq helped carve out a dominant role for the state in the postrevolutionary economy. In the immediate aftermath, this was at least in part a response to the enormous dislocation spawned by the revolution. Factories ground to a halt as a result of labor strikes and fleeing owners. University students took over hotels, and poor Tehranis simply moved themselves into the homes of the wealthy.[70] They were provoked and organized by radicals who created a network to identify, occupy, and distribute property in hopes of accelerating the transfer of power and undercutting the moderate provisional government. To consolidate support for the system and outmaneuver leftist rivals, Khomeini and his allies began articulating a stronger appeal to poor Iranians, or mostazafan. Khomeini also softened his defense of private property, tacitly sanctioning the wave of expropriations. All these trends intensified

---

68. Ervand Abrahamian, *Khomeinism: Essays on the Islamic Republic* (London: I.B. Tauris, 1993), 39–40.

69. Guilain Denoeux has analyzed the role of the bazaar during the prerevolutionary mobilization. See Denoeux, *Urban Unrest in the Middle East: A Comparative Study of Informal Networks in Egypt, Iran, and Lebanon* (Albany: State University of New York Press, 1993).

70. For an excellent overview of the role of the urban poor in reconfiguring the postrevolutionary economy, see Asef Bayat, *Street Politics: Poor People's Movements in Iran* (New York: Columbia University Press, 1997).

after the Iraqi invasion in September 1980, and for the subsequent eight years the state fully mobilized the nation's resources in support of the war effort.

Article 44 of the Constitution divides the economy into three sectors: public, private, and cooperative, and this provision accords the state monopolies over heavy industry, foreign trade, banking, insurance, energy and other mineral resource development, and communication and transportation infrastructure. Khomeini's shift leftward did not wholly override his innate conservatism on economic issues but simply perpetuated the bitter dispute within the regime. Vociferous debates over proposals to nationalize foreign trade, subsidize basic consumer goods, and other economic issues deadlocked the parliament during its early years, and nearly fractured the instrumental alliance with the bazaaris. Iran's Council of Guardians, which is empowered to vet parliamentary legislation, consistently favored a more conservative interpretation of sharia and routinely rejected aggressive measures on land reform and the nationalization of foreign trade.[71]

While this populist rhetoric has never extended to a broad restructuring of Iran's social structures, the dueling approaches toward the economy left an ambiguous legacy for the market in Iran. The fundamental problem in Iran has not been state ownership so much as it has been state intervention in the rational functioning of the market. "Over time, substantial and entrenched price distortions developed in the economy, with serious consequences at all levels of economic activity from investment to production, trade, distribution, and consumption."[72] The consequences include excessive bureaucracy, price controls and vast subsidies, import and export restrictions, a dominant state role in the economy, an anemic private sector, an arbitrary tax regime, corruption, and rigid labor laws.

After Khomeini's 1989 death, Rafsanjani assumed the newly empowered post of president and Khamenei succeeded Khomeini as supreme leader. Both were senior Islamic Republic officials throughout its first decade and were identified with the conservative wing of Iran's increasingly fractious partisan squabbling. Rafsanjani's foremost priority was rebuilding an Iran battered by a decade of revolution and war; per capita income had dropped by 45 percent since the revolution, inflation was approaching 29 percent, and total damages from the war (direct and indirect) were somewhere in

---

71. See Bahman Baktiari, *Parliamentary Politics in Revolutionary Iran: The Institutionalization of Factional Politics* (Gainesville: University Press of Florida, 1996) for an overview of the political dimensions. For a description of the ideological underpinnings of this debate, see Saeed Rahnema and Farhad Nomani, *The Secular Miracle: Religion, Politics and Economic Policy in Iran* (London: Zed Press, 1990); Shaul Bakhash, *The Reign of the Ayatollahs: Iran and the Islamic Revolution* (New York: Basic Books, Inc., 1984): 167–75.

72. Hassan Hakimian and Massoud Karshenas, "Dilemmas and Prospects for Economic Reform and Reconstruction in Iran," in *The Economy of Iran: The Dilemmas of an Islamic State,* ed. Parvin Alizadeh (London: I.B. Tauris, 2000), 35.

the neighborhood of $1 trillion.[73] Rafsanjani advocated a fundamental reorientation and liberalization of Iran's economy, along with efforts to reverse Iran's international isolation. This course immediately set him at odds with Islamic leftists in the parliament who remained wedded to the state-centric economic model of the war period and who viewed any embrace of the free market as a betrayal of the revolution's ideals.

After three years of tensions between the president and the parliament over a range of sociocultural issues, Rafsanjani and Khamenei engineered the ouster of left-leaning members of parliament in hopes of facilitating the regime's economic program. They did so by deploying the vetting authority of one of the key clerical oversight bodies, a move that would eventually empower a creeping conservative stranglehold on Iran's elective institutions. Ironically, this effort to consolidate authority and marginalize dissenters did little to accomplish its original objectives. Liberated from his left-wing adversaries, Rafsanjani's second term was stymied by traditional conservatives, prompting the emergence of a third faction that remains relevant to the contestation within the system, the technocrats or pragmatic conservatives.[74]

Moreover, in the absence of meaningful shifts in Iran's foreign policy, Rafsanjani's embrace of market reforms did not ameliorate one of the chief constraints on the Iranian economy—U.S. economic sanctions. Rather, Iran experienced a dramatic intensification of U.S. economic pressure during the latter years of his presidency, triggered by the spectacular backfiring of a gesture intended by Tehran to signal new possibilities for U.S.-Iranian cooperation. In 1995, Iran announced that Conoco, an American firm, would be awarded the country's first upstream oil deal since the revolution, a contract worth approximately $1 billion. The reaction in what was a fiercely contested U.S. political environment was swift and negative, and even after Conoco retreated from the deal, the Clinton administration issued an executive order banning virtually all U.S. trade and investment with Iran. A year later, the Congress enacted secondary sanctions intended to dissuade third countries from investing in Iran's energy sector. The impact of external pressures and internal inconsistencies meant that Rafsanjani left office with a decidedly mixed record of achievement on his signature issue, liberalizing and growing Iran's economy.

For his successor, Iran's economic dilemmas were both ancillary and urgent. During his campaign, Khatami's platform focused almost exclusively

---

73. Anoushiravan Ehteshami, *After Khomeini: The Iranian Second Republic* (London: Routledge, 1995), 93; Jahangir Amuzegar, *Iran's Economy Under the Islamic Republic* (London: I.B. Tauris, 1993), 276, 304.

74. This grouping was formalized during the final years of the Rafsanjani presidency under the banner of *Kargozaran-e Sazandegi* (Servants of the Reconstruction), a caucus led by members of Rafsanjani's cabinet. See Mehdi Moslem, *Factional Politics in Post-Khomeini Iran* (Syracuse, NY: Syracuse University Press, 2002), 130–34.

on sociocultural liberalization, but once in office, he found himself confronted with equally serious problems of economic stagnation and international isolation—compounded by an oil price that had plummeted to less than $10 a barrel. However, relatively few of the reformist leaders wielded strong command over economic issues, and their semisocialist predilections had long positioned them as proponents of a central state role in trade and industry.[75]

Khatami and his allies argued that gradual political change represented the key to resolving Iran's multiple challenges, arguing before an audience of increasingly skeptical students that "Our society faces serious problems and solving those problems requires cooperation and peace and calm. . . . In order to establish minimum stability and development, we have no option but to set the country's economic development at 6 percent and the growth of investment at just above 7 percent in the country. This requires an atmosphere of agreement and cooperation, without tension. We need private investment. We need the private sector's investment. We need foreign facilities. Naturally, with moderation and calm, we can better move on this path."[76]

Beyond their intellectual leanings, this strategy reflected widespread frustration with the Rafsanjani economic agenda. Although Rafsanjani's allies made up an important segment within the reformist leadership, they explicitly rejected his approach, which they saw as having condoned political repression while dispersing little to none of the dividends of reconstruction through growth or enhanced competitiveness. Instead, the reformists argued for strengthening civil society and rule of law, expecting that this progress would create spillover effects on the economy; as an influential reformist journal opined, "It is through this feeling of participation and social cohesion that the economic wheels will start to turn."[77]

The focus on political reform in advance of economic restructuring also reflected the enormous obstacles facing the state. A serious program to promote economic growth and competitiveness would entail dismantling the manifold inefficiencies of the prevailing system—its subsidies, state monopolies, labor safeguards, and overall structural distortions. All of these measures would generate long-term gains but also short-term public pain. For the reformists, who saw public support as their single potent asset, the political costs of undertaking meaningful economic liberalization would have severely threatened their political viability. "If the government loses its popular appeal, it has lost everything," one economic official remarked at

---

75. Of the many excellent books that address the reform movement and the Khatami presidency, one of the best is Ali Ansari's absorbing narrative of its rise and fall. *Iran, Islam and Democracy: The Politics of Managing Change* (London: Royal Institute of International Affairs, 2006).

76. "President Khatami Addresses Students on Reform, Extremism," Islamic Republic News Agency, December 23, 2001.

77. "Obedience or Participation?" *Iran-e Farda* 45 (July–August 1998): 3.

the time. "So the government has to depend on people, and you cannot keep the people in the streets with empty stomachs. . . . So who is going to cut the subsidies?"[78] While Iran's economic predicament in the late 1990s undoubtedly shaped the reform movement—driving, for example, the pursuit of a regional détente and an improved international image—their remedies and rhetoric remained grounded in a sequential approach that prioritized political, social, and cultural initiatives.

The Khatami administration managed to push through a series of small, stepping-stone reforms, including unification of the exchange rate, an improved foreign investment law, and new openings for private and foreign banks. Khatami also succeeded in enhancing transparency and accountability of Iran's *bonyads* (parastatal foundations), including the publication of audited annual reports and taxation of their subsidiary companies. Still, he did not manage to stanch the tide of unemployment, which doubled during his first five years in office.[79] In addition, investment in the nonoil sector remained relatively low outside of the booming construction sector. Privatization proceeded very slowly, and primarily entailed a transfer of ownership from the state sector to a range of semipublic pension and social security funds. Even the relatively favorable conditions in Iran's multiplying free-trade zones tended to foster a thriving export trade and smuggling rather than productive investment.

The reformists' limited success on economic issues, together with their almost complete frustration in institutionalizing political change, paved the way for Ahmadinejad's radical populism. "I like Khatami," one Iranian told the Associated Press on the eve of the president's second term in 2001. "But I'd like him even more if he starts creating some jobs."[80]

Ahmadinejad's populist rhetoric and program—particularly his ostentatious efforts to dispense the state's largesse since taking office—revive themes that were central to the early postrevolutionary period.[81] The resentment that Ahmadinejad's reckless populism has evoked among the conservative elite, evidenced by the parliament's resistance to many of his initiatives as well as the vituperative critiques emanating from his recently ousted oil and industry ministers, demonstrates the continuing salience of the early ideological divide within the postrevolutionary regime.

---

78. Dr. Aliakbar Arabmazar, deputy minister for taxation, interview by author, August 16, 1999.

79. "Economic Practices Undemocratic," *Iran Daily*, May 22, 2002.

80. "Iran's Many Angles on Reform: From Jobs to Dates," Associated Press, June 6, 2001.

81. Abrahamian, *Khomeinism: Essays*; Manoucher Dorraj, *From Zarathustra to Khomeini: Populism and Dissent in Iran* (Boulder: Lynne Rienner, 1990); Dorraj, "Populism and Corporatism in Post-Revolutionary Political Culture," in *Political Culture in the Islamic Republic*, eds. Samih K. Farsoun and Mehrdad Mashayekhi (London: Routledge, 1992).

Iran's resource base has provided a critical buttress for Ahmadinejad's tumultuous presidency, most notably through the windfall revenues of the ongoing oil boom. Tehran is expected to reap a record $70 billion in oil revenues in 2008, and in a system that combines the worst features of rentierism with a socialist planning model, this bounty represents a critical component among the factors that entrench the current system. The state's dominant role in all aspects of the economy sustains elite privileges, and direct state subsidies to the population enable the leadership to buy off potential opposition, at least in part. Predictably, the recent financial influx has only generated a particularly ill-conceived and inflationary economic program, and has apparently stymied any prospects for a serious anticorruption campaign.

Ahmadinejad's economic policies—combined with new U.S. financial measures to pressure the regime, UN Security Council sanctions on key individuals and institutions, and a drop in foreign investment due to the president's provocative rhetoric and increased concerns about political risk—has resulted in even greater distortions for Iran's long-mismanaged economy. Inflation rose dramatically as a result of his free-wheeling spending policies and pressure on state banks to expand lending and lower interest rates, and even the questionable official rate now tops 19 percent. The banking restrictions imposed by Washington have greatly complicated the mechanisms of international trade, raising costs and resulting in project delays. In 2006 and 2007, more than fifty of the country's most prominent economic experts issued public letters criticizing Ahmadinejad's approach in exquisite detail, warning that "With the continuation of these hasty and nonexpert decisions it is feared that the national economy would face even a more difficult situation, and with the passage of time the cost of getting out of the looming economic crises would become heavier for the people and for the economic managers of the country."[82]

Ahmadinejad's assiduous deployment of economic issues makes him especially vulnerable to the regime's stumbling in this area. The president has rejected the criticism, implicating his predecessors for the problems he is trying to resolve and suggesting that his critics simply resent losing access to their privileged place in Iran's economy. "A certain few should not grab the country's resources and hold them," he admonished in a 2006 speech on the state of the economy. "And, as soon as one tries to stop them, there is a hue and cry. They say that Ahmadinejad knows nothing about economics. Yes, if that means that I know nothing about economics, I pray to God that I will never know about economics—the kind of economics that means grabbing

---

82. "The Second Warning of the Economists to the Administration," *Etemad*, June 12, 2007, www.etemaad.com/Released/86-03-22/150.htm#29791 (accessed May 9, 2008).

the people's money and not paying it back, when a certain group takes it and the majority are deprived of it. We will prevent that."[83]

The most immediate political consequence of Ahmadinejad's economic policies has been an intensification of factional contention within the Islamic Republic's elites. Ahmadinejad's boasts in early 2007 about the bargain price of tomatoes in his low-rent Tehran neighborhood sparked a furious backlash in the parliament and from other Iranian power brokers, as well as a flurry of popular jokes at his expense. Reformists have tried to exploit public frustration with the economic circumstances, while some of the impact has hit hardest on the conservatives' traditional base of support in the merchant class. As a result, the debate over Iran's economic policies has intensified greatly, particularly because the oil boom inevitably raises public expectations for a trickle-down effect. "In the last two years, oil, which should have been the harbinger of transformations in our country, has led to the lowering of our ranking in terms of the degree of ease of carrying out trade and business," former nuclear negotiator Hassan Ruhani lamented. "Even countries like Pakistan, the Republic of Azerbaijan, Bangladesh, and Nigeria are ahead of us in that table, and this shows that if the planning is not correct, even expensive oil will not be able to save us."[84]

The uproar among Iran's insiders reflects a well-justified hypersensitivity to public opinion. Across the spectrum, Iranian political actors are well aware that the system's legitimacy and stability are fundamentally interconnected with the popular sense of well-being and security. Iranian officials also recognize the escalatory potential of the country's persistent, although still relatively sporadic, labor unrest in recent years in Tehran and other major cities, including Hamadan, Ilam, Ahwaz, Bandar Abbas, Kashan, Yazd, Shiraz, and the province of Hormuzgan. "Though still in formative stages, and not entirely outside the control of the state, collective actions around unpaid wages and labor rights increased in number in 1998 and 1999."[85] Some of the largest and most sustained demonstrations have been organized by Iranian teachers, who are paid a paltry $100 a month; in 2002, three thousand teachers rallied in front of Khatami's office as he met with visiting UN secretary-general Kofi Annan.[86] More recently, the 2005 arrest of Mansour Ossanlu, the leader of the Tehran bus drivers' union, has generated an ongo-

---

83. President Mahmoud Ahmadinejad, speech on the state of the economy given August 14, 2006, broadcast by Vision of the Islamic Republic of Iran Network 1, translated by BBC Monitoring.

84. "Ruhani: Societies That Make Up Enemies Always Fail—Cannot Eliminate Rivals," *Farhang-e Ashti*, November 22, 2007, www.ashtidaily.com/Detail.aspx?cid=119783&catid=491 (accessed May 9, 2008).

85. Yaghmaian, *Social Change in Iran*, 2002, 23.

86. Afshin Valinejad, "Protest Mars Annan Visit to Tehran," Associated Press, January 26, 2002.

ing cycle of demonstrations that garnered significant international attention; Ossanlu was arrested for a third time in July 2007.

Regional Developments

Another obvious force for change is the almost unprecedented fluidity that has come to characterize the Middle East over the past several years, both with respect to regional relationships and internal controls. The Middle East was long known for its resistance to change and tendency toward ossification; for better *and* for worse, all that has changed. These changes can be attributed, at least in part, to the Bush administration's self-branded "transformational diplomacy"—most significantly, the decision to use military force to remove Saddam Hussein from power, but also American efforts to cultivate democratic transitions in the region. These U.S. policies are having immense reverberations across the region and within states and societies—impacts that are still not clear or fully understood.

These dynamics create considerable uncertainty for the endurance of the Iranian regime. First and foremost, the regional instability sparked intense anxieties, both within Iran and more broadly in the international community, that Washington was bent on replacing the Iranian regime by force or intervention. The Bush administration cultivated this perception, initially based on the hubristic assumption that the Islamic Republic was on the verge of collapse or implosion.

In addition, there is the "Sistani factor." The aging, reclusive Grand Ayatollah Ali Sistani has proved himself to be the single most powerful individual in post-Saddam Iraq—able to reshape the vast bureaucratic apparatus of the postwar U.S. administration and set a new political course for Iraqis of all ethnic and religious backgrounds—all without leaving his office or engaging directly with Americans. His legitimacy and proven independence endows Sistani with considerable influence, and his ethnic Persian heritage provides him with particular affinities for Iran as well as Iraq. According to Iraq expert Yitzakh Nakash, "during the Iran-Iraq war, Sistani managed to demonstrate that he could be controlled neither by Saddam nor by his fellow ayatollahs in Iran, which has given him enormous credibility."[87]

Sistani ranks as a marja-ye taqlid. He follows the traditionally quietist school of Shia thought, generally opposing the involvement of the clergy in the day-to-day affairs of government. But—not wholly dissimilar to Khomeini—his view of his own responsibilities has gradually expanded to fit the circumstances in which he and his country now find themselves. In this way, Sistani has become an unexpected and unrelenting advocate of democracy and independence as the irreversible bases for the new Iraqi political order.

---

87. Fareed Zakaria, "An Absence of Legitimacy," *Washington Post*, January 20, 2004.

This position—as well as the restraint that Sistani has persistently urged Iraqis to demonstrate in response to violence and provocations—sets Iraq's most prominent ayatollah at considerable variance from his counterparts within the Islamic Republic. Moreover, Sistani's experience and scholarship elevates his authority among believers far beyond the comparatively modest credentials of Iran's politicized clerical leader, Ayatollah Khamenei. Conscious perhaps of this gap and wary of widening his appeal at home or inciting nationalist resentment among Iraqis, Iranian officials have taken care not to undermine Sistani's role or his edicts. Sistani has yet to address Iran's political dynamics directly and is extremely unlikely to do so. Still, his forceful defense of a more democratic outcome in Iraq will inevitably reverberate among Iranians and could intensify the long-standing opposition within an important segment of the clergy to the velayet-e faqih principle of Islamic rule. Iranian clerics have quickly recognized the potential competition, and some—including dissident cleric Ayatollah Montazeri—have already endeavored to align themselves with Sistani and reach out to Iraq's Shia community.[88]

Related to the Sistani factor is the reemergence of Najaf and Karbala as the preeminent places of Shia religious learning and pilgrimage, a status that the two cities held for centuries until Saddam Hussein's repression largely cut off Iraq's clergy from the wider Muslim world. Ayatollah Khomeini studied in Najaf and later spent twelve years in exile there; until the 1980s, most other distinguished clergy would have also engaged in their formative education there. As Graham Fuller has noted, "the several holy Shiite cities of Iraq have produced a flowering of Shiite culture and thought that is central to Shiism as a whole."[89] By comparison, Iran's theological center—Qom—was still somewhat peripheral to the great debates of Islamic jurisprudence; it boasted a briefer history and far fewer pilgrims until the postrevolutionary government began to invest in its development. Thanks to the countervailing political dynamics in the two neighbors, Qom has flourished over the past twenty-five years, while Najaf has shrunk to a fraction of its former size and influence.

Regime change in Iraq has reopened its sanctuaries and seminaries to the broader Islamic community, although security concerns have temporarily stemmed the flow of pilgrims. Not surprisingly, Iran's religious establishment has responded to the possible challenge from Iraq in opportunistic fashion. According to Qom-based cleric and writer Mohammad Javad Akbarein, "The Qom seminary wants to remain as a pioneer platform for Shiite Islamic thinking and definitely doesn't want Najaf to take its place."[90] In an

88. "Iran's Dissident Cleric Calls on People to Vote," Associated Press, December 23, 2004.

89. Fuller, Center of the Universe, 38.

90. Hamza Hendawi, "Shiite Leadership Clash in Iran, Iraq," Associated Press, July 15, 2004.

effort apparently intended to establish a clerical network that is beholden to Tehran, in the early months following the fall of Saddam, Iranian clerics offered stipends to Iraqi seminarians in Qom to return home and preach on short stints.[91]

The argument that the revival of Najaf would pose an inherent threat to Iran's Islamic order was widely accepted in Washington during the early days after the U.S. intervention in Iraq. As Ali Allawi writes, "This was a highly simplistic and misleading reading of Shia religious institutions and the interaction within the religious hierarchies of the Shia world."[92] To date, Allawi's analysis has proved far more prescient than the ill-informed American conventional wisdom. However, just as the liberation of Iraq's holy places has not come at the detriment of Qom or religious authority in Iran, it is also clear that the resurgence of Iraqi religious institutions offers some long-term potential for fostering constructive change in Iran. As a consequence of the revolution, Qom remains "very politicized"[93] and nationalistic. Moreover, while reformist theologians such as Mohsen Kadivar and Mohammad Mojtahed-Shabestari have carved out a small niche in Qom, most of Iran's clerical networks are marked by top-down enforcement of ideological conformity with the basic principles of the state, including velayet-e faqih. Renewing the historical trends of cross-fertilization between the Persian and Arab clergy might help to counterbalance those trends and foster a broader and more innovative public debate on the appropriate relationship between the state and religion. While debates among seminarians can hardly be expected to generate meaningful political change in the short term, Iran's recent history demonstrates that some of the most persuasive—and therefore dangerous, from the point of view of the authorities—opponents of the current political system are those who can effectively rebut the regime's reliance on its presumptive divine mandate.

Beyond the ferment among the Shia populations of both countries, the recent political turmoil in Iraq has generated other potential triggers for change within Iran. For example, it appears to have helped reactivate a long dormant sectarian conflict in southern Iran, whose Arab population and—not coincidentally—sizeable oil resources have historically attracted claims by various Iraqi governments.[94] In April 2005, false reports of a government plan to relocate large numbers of non-Arabs to the port city of Ahvaz in order to alter its ethnic make-up sparked serious protests that quickly devolved into violence. Three people were killed and two hundred arrested as demonstrators set fire

91. Peyman Pejman, "Iran Sends Iraqis Home to Preach," *Washington Times*, July 8, 2003.
92. Ali A. Allawi, *The Occupation of Iraq: Winning the War, Losing the Peace* (New Haven: Yale University Press, 2007), 311.
93. Hendawi, "Shiite Leadership Clash."
94. Hunter, "Outlook for Iranian-Gulf Relations," 437.

to public buildings. A previously unknown separatist group subsequently demanded an end to Iran's "occupation" of the Arab-majority province of Khuzestan. Since then, Iran's political dynamics and regional interactions have created new uncertainties for other minority populations, particularly the Balouch.

Another unintended consequence of U.S. policy toward Iraq over the past fifteen years has been the cultivation of political autonomy and cultural re-surgence among the region's Kurds. Twelve years of no-fly zones gave Iraq's Kurdish population its first opportunity to experiment with self-rule and positioned their leaders to play a formidable role in the post-Saddam jockey-ing for power. It also intensified the development of a distinct Kurdish cul-tural identity, expressed in print and broadcast media, universities, and civil society organizations and disseminated via new satellite television stations throughout Iraq and to coethnics in Turkey, Syria, and Iran. These trends may or may not have been exacerbated by covert operations reportedly un-dertaken by Israel in Iraqi Kurdistan in support of forces that oppose the Iranian government.[95]

The political and cultural ascendance of Iraqi Kurds appeared to inten-sify some of the long-standing grievances among Iran's 6 million Kurds, who make up approximately 7 percent of Iran's total population. With a history of activism dating back to the post–World War II period, Iranian Kurds have long been prone to nationalist agitation. In the aftermath of the Islamic Revo-lution, the new regime in Tehran battled a low-level insurgency in Kurdistan waged by Kurdish rebels who enjoyed considerable local support. As part of this troubled history of integration in the Iranian state, Kurds have long expressed cultural and religious grievances (most Iranian Kurds are Sunni Muslims). Although conditions for Iran's minorities generally improved dur-ing the eight years of Khatami's presidency, this period also corresponded to increasing activism among Iranian Kurds. A Kurdish MP condemned the government in 2000 for conducting a "campaign of repression, serial mur-ders, and the banning of the faith" against Sunni Kurds, and in September 2001, the six MPs representing Iran's Kurdistan province attempted to re-sign en masse over concerns about discrimination against their coethnics, although the Majlis rejected their resignation letter.[96]

This pattern of disturbances appears to have been intensified by the changes in the region. Small-scale unrest has been reported in several pre-dominantly Kurdish cities in the Islamic Republic since the fall of the Sad-dam Hussein regime. In March 2004, a Kurdish member of Iran's Majlis told a Western news service that "residents of several Kurdish towns have taken

---

95. Seymour M. Hersh, "Israel Looks to the Kurds," *New Yorker*, June 28, 2004.
96. "Kurdish MP Accuses Iran's Regime of Repression, Murders," Agence France-Presse, No-vember 28, 2000.

to the street to show their joy and their solidarity with the Iraqi Kurds, who have gained the right of autonomy after years of repression."[97] Clashes reportedly occurred once again in June 2005, when security forces attempted to break up celebrations among nationalist Kurds over the election of Jalal Talabani, leader of the Iraqi Patriotic Union of Kurdistan, as president of Iraq's interim government, and again the following month after the reported shooting of a Kurdish separatist activist. The violence is especially worrying because it dovetails with other evidence of the poor integration of Kurds into the Islamic state. The province of Kurdistan registered the lowest levels of voter turnout across the nation in the June 2005 presidential election, with only 25 percent of the electorate participating in the ballot (versus a national turnout rate of approximately 60 percent.)

There are, of course, other influences that the regional environment may have on Iran's internal situation. Senior U.S. officials have pointed repeatedly to the political progress under way in several other Middle Eastern states, notably Afghanistan, Egypt, Lebanon, Iraq, and the Palestinian territories, suggesting that these trends may encourage Iranians to press their own government more aggressively. A preelection statement by President Bush noted that "[a]cross the Middle East, hopeful change is taking place. People are claiming their liberty. And as a tide of freedom sweeps this region, it will also come eventually to Iran."[98] Both sides of the political aisle in Washington began comparing the sudden evidence of domestic ferment and its consequences to Eastern Europe on the eve of the collapse of communism.[99]

The potential ripple effect on Iran of democratic developments in any one of these countries is difficult to ascertain. It is not hard to imagine that positive news emanating from other Middle Eastern capitals may encourage many Iranians to view both the process of their recent elections—which was flawed and manipulated in unprecedented ways, even by the standards of past elections in the Islamic Republic—and its outcome as Secretary of State Rice described it, "thoroughly out of step with what is going on in the larger region."[100] Such a perception could well intensify Iranians' demands for greater political participation and other reforms. Given the distinct national identity and sense of superiority that tends to color Iranians' views of their country and the world, however, it is not clear that Iran's electorate will adopt this comparative perspective, or that if they did, they would necessarily see

97. "Scores of Iranian Kurds Arrested after Demo," Agence France-Presse, March 11, 2004.

98. Robin Wright and Michael A. Fletcher, "Bush Denounces Iran's Election," *Washington Post*, June 17, 2005.

99. See, for example, the statements of Senator Joseph Lieberman in Todd S. Purdum, "For Bush, No Boasts, but a Taste of Vindication," *New York Times*, March 9, 2005.

100. Secretary of State Condoleezza Rice, interview by Charlie Rose, *Charlie Rose Show*, PBS, June 9, 2005, www.state.gov/secretary/rm/2005/47616.htm (accessed April 17, 2008).

their own situation as profoundly inferior to the overall political context in, for example, Iraq, Afghanistan, or Palestine.

Women and Technology

In Iran today, there are a number of issues and uncertainties beyond those with the greatest potential for catalyzing change that pose some prospect for influencing the future course of the state. Iranian history suggests the salience of narrow mobilization for shaping the broader societal dynamics. For example, in 1977, a program of ten nights of poetry readings represented the first salvo of the revolution and provided venues for the educated, emerging middle class to discuss political ideas and make connections with the more traditional communities of the bazaari and the working class, which had already moved on to more drastic measures of opposing the Shah.[101] The limitations on these groups were clear and significant, and yet their very existence helped give shape to the demands of their constituencies and form the basis for a multipronged opposition to the monarchy. In the current political dynamics, it is possible to imagine that several disparate factors—women and the proliferation of communication technologies—could have a similar dramatic impact on Iran's political future.

Since the outset of the revolution, women have been a key constituency for the regime, and the panoply of issues associated with women's place in society has served as a key barometer for Iran's political climate. During the lead-up to the revolution, the veil was eagerly embraced by some Iranian women (and men) as a stark, silent objection to the regime, just as the miniskirt symbolized the decadence and cultural alienation associated with the monarchy's infatuation with the West. During this period, women schemed to sneak their chadors—proscribed by the Shah—onto university campuses, and the headscarf effectively became required garb for participation in revolutionary demonstrations.[102] Shortly after Khomeini's 1979 return to Iran, however, fierce opposition to the consolidation of clerical authority emerged from the ranks of Iran's women. Although the

---

101. Azadeh Kian-Thiébaut, *Secularization of Iran a Doomed Failure? The New Middle Class and the Making of Modern Iran* (Paris: Peeters, 1998), 148–69.

102. One of the many ironies of the Iranian revolution involves the extent to which its negative impact on the status of women has tended to focus the eye of Western scholarship on this subject, thereby generating a rich body of valuable literature (as well, of course, as ideologically motivated diatribes). For several recent examples of this scholarship, see Ziba Mir-Hosseini, *Islam and Gender: The Religious Debate in Contemporary Iran* (Princeton, NJ: Princeton University Press, 1999); Haleh Afshar, *Islam and Feminism: An Iranian Case-Study* (New York: St. Martin's Press, 1998); Parvin Paidar, *Women and the Political Process in Twentieth-Century Iran* (Cambridge: Cambridge University Press, 1995); and Haideh Moghissi, *Populism and Feminism in Iran: Women's Struggle in a Male-Defined Revolutionary Movement* (New York: St. Martin's Press, 1994).

revolutionary mobilization offered new opportunities for political activism and leadership among women, its aftermath left their social, political, and legal status significantly degraded.[103]

The turning point for Iranian women came on March 6, 1979, in remarks by Ayatollah Khomeini calling for enforcement of Islamic dress. This provoked an outpouring of protest on the day after the news was reported, which happened to coincide with International Women's Day (March 8). This represented the "first powerful challenge to Khomeini's authority,"[104] and sufficiently spooked the clerics that they backed away from this mandate until they gained a tighter grip on power more than a year later. This incident itself is properly assigned a relatively minor significance in the annals of the Islamic Republic's history. After all, the threat of female activism did not forestall the immediate (February 1979) abrogation of the 1975 Family Protection Act, the key legal basis for women's civil and family rights under the monarchy, nor a host of other regressive modifications to the legal, political, and cultural realm for women in the Islamic Republic.[105] While it is important not to overstate the organizational or ideological coherence of the women's movement at this time, the March 1979 mobilization against Khomeini's edict, and the reaction by the clerical authorities, highlights the deep divisions within the revolutionary coalition as well as the significance of feminist opposition to the Islamic state.[106]

Over the course of the regime's history, women have remained an active force, never more so than since the election of Ahmadinejad. Their cause has been furthered by the crackdown on enforcement of Islamic dress codes

---

103. See the testimony by one female activist in Hammed Shahidian, "Women and Clandestine Politics in Iran, 1970–1985," *Feminist Studies* 23, no. 1 (Spring 1997): 7–42.

104. Haideh Moghissi, *Populism and Feminism in Iran: Women's Struggle in a Male-Defined Revolutionary Movement* (New York: St. Martin's Press, 1994), 140–43.

105. Once again, a brief caveat: as before the revolution, women in the Islamic Republic continue to play active roles in Iran's politics, participate fully in its educational system, and engage in meaningful employment and cultural activities without the drastic social constraints imposed by governments in other countries of the Persian Gulf. This is another common misimpression that bears comment. At the same time, the inequities in the family law, in particular, as well as other restrictions within the political system, are severely detrimental to women and are the focus of today's activism among Iranian women. See Ziba Mir-Hosseini, *Marriage on Trial: A Study of Islamic Family Law: Iran and Morocco Compared* (London: I.B. Tauris, 1993).

106. Notwithstanding the comments in the previous note, it appears that the issue of hijab (modest dress) generates a more profound sense of political urgency, both from the regime and from feminist activists, than perhaps more substantive issues such as legal reform. General laxity about hijab as a result of broader political changes gave rise to a new series of regulations on veiling in 1989, and the spontaneous jubilation at Iran's qualification for the 1998 World Cup—which involved public dancing and unveiling—generated much greater interest than commensurate developments in the legal or political realm. In fact, it is said that the very rumor that the chador might be mandated under his administration helped to doom the 1997 presidential candidacy of then speaker of the parliament Ali Akbar Nateq Nouri, despite his protestations to the contrary. For Nateq Nouri's denials of this rumor, see "Election Update," *Tehran Times*, May 21, 1997, and "Last Minute Campaigning in the Provinces Seeks to Scoop Votes," *Iran News*, May 20, 1997.

and social standards under Ahmadinejad; one recent sweep by the security forces resulted in more than 150,000 women stopped in Tehran for "bad *hejab*" or insufficient veiling in a single month.[107] An Internet drive organized by several female Iranian activists that was intended to press for equality for women under Iranian law known as the "Million Signatures Campaign" helped spark one of the few episodes of organized popular dissent during the early Ahmadinejad years. Small rallies held in Tehran in June 2005 and 2006 designed to highlight the campaign garnered only a handful of participants, but the government's overwhelming response helped to generate an enormous amount of international publicity and a cyclical series of demonstrations, arrests, and further confrontations with the regime.[108] Some analysts suggested that this renewed women's activism could serve as a leading edge for a more broad-based opposition campaign. One scholar noted the irony "that in a male-dominated culture it is the women who are mainly gathering to express political dissidence, and who are motivating reformist men to follow them in their demonstrations."[109]

Technology represents yet another potential vehicle for facilitating political change. The social and political retrenchment of the Ahmadinejad era has only heightened the significance of the Internet as a medium of political expression and, potentially, mobilization as well. Iran's Internet usage has undergone "the most explosive growth of the countries in the Middle East, with an increase of 2,900 percent between 2000 and 2005."[110] This accelerated development was aided in part by the lack of significant restrictions on the technology in its early years of adoption in Iran. In fact, until 2003, the Iranian regime "encouraged the expansion of the Internet" and only episodically endeavored to exert control over either the technology or the content—notably, a radical distinction from its approach to other communications technology, such as satellite technology.

Pathways to Change

Given these various pressures—and the likelihood for any number of unforeseen developments to influence the future course of the country— Iran appears to have reached a critical turning point, from which two divergent alternative paths can be identified. Either scenario for Iran's

---

107. Borzou Daragahi, "Iran Tightens Screws on Internal Dissent," *Los Angeles Times*, June 10, 2007.

108. Ziba Mir-Hosseini, "Is Time on Iranian Women Protesters' Side?" *Middle East Report Online*, June 16, 2006.

109. Majid Mohammadi, "When Women are the Real Men in Iran," *Daily Star* (Beirut), March 27, 2007.

110. Profile of Iran by OpenNet Initiative, http://opennet.net/sites/opennet.net/files/iran.pdf (accessed April 17, 2008); see also "Internet Filtering in Iran: 2004-2005," http://opennet. net/studies/iran/ONI_Country_Study_Iran.pdf (accessed April 17, 2008).

future begins with the surprising and profoundly ambiguous presidential election that reversed Iran's recent domestic political trend toward popular support for the forces of democratic, liberal change. On the one hand, the election of Ahmadinejad seems to have signaled the consolidation and retrenchment of the Islamic Republic, empowered and emboldened by high oil revenues, the limitations on U.S. military power, and the increasing role of Russia and China as alternative power centers in the international system. Alternatively, the current period may prove to be precisely the critical juncture that generates sufficient popular pressure to bring about the sort of meaningful political change that Iranians have demanded. Under this more optimistic future, Ahmadinejad's provocative policies and the regime's failure to redress the fundamental distortions that plague the economy would galvanize the development of a robust and effective opposition. Either scenario would mean a conspicuous readjustment of Iran's policies and interactions with the Islamic world, as discussed below.

This analysis began with the basic assumption that the paradigm of "change from within" enunciated by Khatami and his reformist allies over the past eight years is essentially bankrupt. That implies that any kind of meaningful political change will require some pressure on Iran's existing political system from its own population. Internal pressure indisputably exists; fundamentally, the election of Ahmadinejad reflects the profound and utter disappointment with the Iranian electorate, both in their government as well as the forces who endeavored to change it gradually during the late 1990s. However, for that pressure to be effective in cultivating political change, several basic conditions must be present.

First, Iran's dissatisfied population needs a tenacious leader. Iran is replete with dissidents—individuals who have testified eloquently through their work and their writings to the need for change, many of whom have suffered for that cause. Among the most prominent are the writer Akbar Ganji and Ayatollah Hussein Ali Montazeri. However, as any comparative survey of revolutionary movements will attest, dissidents do not always make effective or compelling leaders of a mass-based opposition movement. To successfully press their case for change, the foes of Iran's regime will need a cadre of activists who can rally followers, marshal resources, and develop and implement a specific program to effect that change. The reformist movement had a profusion of talented strategists, including Said Hajjarian who was seriously injured in an assassination attempt in February 2000; it is unclear if any of those operatives or politicians who heretofore preferred to work within the system can successfully transition to a leading role in the opposition.

In addition to a leader, Iran's opposition needs both an organization and a strategy. As the reformists learned—repeatedly and to their own detriment—the lack of any organized mechanism to channel popular frustration will undermine any prospect of effectiveness. The reformists' own vehicle, the Islamic Iran Participation Front (Mosharekat), never became a functioning political party; until the end of their tenure in government, Mosharekat remained an elite debating society, with no capacity to mobilize the population or advance its political agenda. Loose associations of like-minded intellectuals will not be sufficient to coordinate Iran's inchoate forces of democratic opposition or to advance their cause successfully.

A strategy is another essential element of political change in Iran that is currently lacking. Iran's opposition forces have some sense of the end state they are seeking, but they have not articulated persuasively how they intend to achieve that. This is particularly true of those who advocate holding a referendum to change Iran's constitution and eliminate clerical authority and oversight. This is undoubtedly a worthy goal; however, the goal itself is explicitly unattainable because it would require the approval of the very political forces that it is intended to eliminate. "Today they are talking about the referendum," Khatami told students in December 2001. "Didn't the people say what they wanted through their participation in the presidential elections, the parliamentary elections, the city-village council elections, and even the recent Golestan province by-elections. . . ? If there are people who do not want to comply with the wishes of the people and all these referendums, they would not give in to the would-be referendum either."[111] Its proponents still have not offered an action plan for realizing this objective. After the past eight years, Iranians are justifiably skeptical of political movements that offer more words than deeds.

An opposition strategy need not be a step-by-step diagram; it can and should be adaptable and open-ended. However, it should entail some basic agreement on a vision for the future; as the Islamic Revolution itself demonstrates, utilitarian cooperation among disparate forces can result in divergent aims and open conflict. For Iran's current opposition forces, this may require some additional consensus building, particularly on the question of secular democracy and what that really means. The experience of the past eight years appears to have generated greater convergence around this issue, but the differences among those seeking political change should be explored and acknowledged.

One final basic condition must develop before meaningful political change or reform can realistically be expected in Iran. There will need to be some willingness on the part of Iranians to press their claims through means that transcend or violate the current rules of the political game in Iran. To date, the fundamental shortcoming hampering Iran's democratic aspirations has been the general unwillingness of Iranians to risk their lives and livelihoods to demand the change they want or to defend the dissidents who have

---

111. "President Khatami Addresses Students on Reform, Extremism," Islamic Republic News Agency, December 23, 2001.

been imprisoned for their own advocacy. To be sure, the Islamic Republic has very effective means of repression at its disposal. However, fear alone cannot explain the lack of opposition action, since Iran also has experienced regular protests and demonstrations without the regime resorting to mass violence. The disinclination of Iranians to mobilize on a mass basis reflects a widespread aversion to unrest and violent change. This is an understandable, if unfortunate, legacy of the Islamic Revolution, but until and unless that sentiment changes, Iran is unlikely to experience meaningful political reforms.

There are, of course, several potential wild cards of tremendous significance. One is the continuing health of the supreme leader, who functions as the linchpin of the current system. If Khamenei were removed from the scene, the process of selecting and seating his replacement could well open up new fissures within the political elite and create new opportunities to subvert the current political system. While political reforms have been few and far between, the social context within Iran has changed dramatically since 1989, the last time the gerontocracy that is the Assembly of Experts gathered to anoint a new leader. And under the current circumstances, it is difficult to imagine that such a transition could be smoothly managed without public input or disapprobation.

Another uncertainty for Iran's political development is the prospect of some catalyzing event. Hariri's assassination played just such a role in Lebanon, galvanizing widespread popular and international opposition to Syrian troop presence into sudden and sustained public action. The "color revolutions" of Ukraine and Georgia offer similar examples whereby an unexpected transgression by an overconfident political system rouses the public's inveterate discontent. It is entirely conceivable that some unforeseen development could shock Iranians into a more assertive push for political change, but it is of course impossible to predict just what event might have such a profound impact. Several past events—including the December 1998 revelations of the "serial murders" of writers and dissidents and the July 1999 student protests—have served as critical junctures, albeit to a lesser extent. However, to date Iranians have demonstrated a high degree of forbearance for the failings and excesses of the Islamic regime.

Implications for the Islamic World

Iran's future course will inevitably pose direct and significant consequences for its relations with the wider Muslim world. The desired end state for U.S. policy and for most Iranians—a democratic Iran that protects the rights of all its citizens—would generally occasion a reduction of tensions between Tehran and its neighbors. It would presumably conclude or deemphasize those policy initiatives that are primarily a function of Iran's revolutionary ideology and its effort to project an Islamist identity. A democratic Iran would have little incentive to engage in or facilitate financial or material support for terrorism, although it would likely struggle to control rogue clerical institutions that might endeavor to retain influence over Hezbollah and other militant groups. By curtailing its official involvement with violent efforts to oppose the Middle East peace process, Iran would reduce, at least in some small way, the popular pressure on other Islamic governments to adopt intransigent positions vis-à-vis that ongoing conflict.

Of course, a democratic Iran would not necessarily be an entirely positive development for the Muslim world. Some other states—Saudi Arabia in particular—may be little assuaged by a stable, confident Iran that was well positioned to develop strong relations with the United States, as well as the rest of the world. Their own status might then be relegated to that lower tier of interest that prevailed during the robust U.S.-Iranian alliance of the 1960s and 1970s.[112] Dubai's thriving economy would eventually cede some of its substantial Iranian capital and investments to a presumably increasingly attractive domestic market. An unreformed government in Baku also might not welcome free and fair elections promoted by its neighbor to the south. Moreover, some of Iran's most provocative policies—including its contested claim to the three Persian Gulf islands and, arguably at least, its nuclear ambitions—can be traced to nationalist imperatives that predate the revolution and might not be substantially altered by the demise of the Islamic Republic. Still, from an objective point of view, a democratic Iran could be expected to greatly enhance the security of the Muslim world.

The alternative scenario for Iran's future development—political regression, cultural orthodoxy, and economic stagnation—would bode more poorly for the wider Muslim world. Theological ferment within Iran's seminaries would presumably grind to a halt; the region's most advanced indigenous debate on the nature of sovereignty and the limitations of divine mandates would also feel the chill of intensified government repression. A retrenching Islamic Republic might reinvigorate the rhetoric, if not the actual policies, of the early years of the revolution, as the advocates of exporting the revolution would presumably find themselves in political ascendance. Whatever factors currently constrain Iranian troublemaking in Iraq could well be loosened, bringing the government into increasingly direct conflict with its neighbors and with the United States. In order to mobilize the regime's waning base of popular support, the leadership would likely seek opportunities to exploit Iran's deep-seated nationalism. Should Iran's political circumstances degenerate, its immediate neighbors would be most directly and immedi-

---

112. In Kahwaji, "U.S.-Arab Cooperation," the author makes precisely this argument in his consideration of the view of the Gulf toward change in Iran.

ately impacted by the prospect of instability and/or state aggression along their borders, but the wider community of Muslim states would also experience some repercussions as well. The ripple effects of a destabilized and deteriorating Iran—as well as from the response of Washington and the Gulf states—could exacerbate violence between Israelis and Palestinians and create new pressures for far-flung states with small but readily mobilized Muslim minorities.

A secondary scenario for concern could come during whatever transition period Iran may experience. If Iran's internal politics become more contentious, the impact may be felt in its external relations in a variety of potentially contradictory ways. Under pressure, the government might be tempted to lash out in an effort to redirect public passions; an international crisis—even a manufactured one—has a powerful way of distracting from day-to-day politics. In such a scenario, the Iranian government might actively engage in a more provocative foreign policy in hopes of mobilizing nationalism in response to some international crisis. As detailed above, Iran wields enormous and varied influence in several Muslim countries of key interest to the United States and could ratchet up pressure in Afghanistan, Iraq, and/or Lebanon. Unfortunately, along Iran's road to political reform, there is much room for its approach to the Muslim world (as well as to the United States) to worsen before it ultimately improves.

4

U.S. Policy toward Iran

Iran ranks as America's most durable foreign policy dilemma. Over the past twenty-nine years, U.S. policy has focused on addressing the threat posed by Tehran. Times—and governments—have changed, but the United States and Iran remain squarely at odds on such critical issues as terrorism and weapons of mass destruction. With U.S. forces now positioned along Iran's borders, Washington's forward challenge will be to foster responsible Iranian conduct toward its neighbors as well as toward its own citizenry.

President George W. Bush sought a comprehensive approach toward Tehran, one that deals with the multiple issues of U.S. concern, including Iran's nuclear ambitions, its bankrolling of terrorism, its bid to assert itself as a regional hegemon, and its repression of its own citizenry. The U.S. strategy was intended to present Iranian leaders with a stark choice between moderation or isolation, and for a period Washington enjoyed unprecedented success in persuading a wide coalition of allies and international actors to support its efforts. Iran itself contributed greatly to uniting the world against it, thanks to Ahmadinejad's truculent rhetoric and the steady expansion of Iranian influence across the region.

Despite achieving unprecedented international consensus, the latest U.S. strategy on Iran has borne little fruit. Iran's nuclear program has advanced with alacrity, and its influence in Iraq and Afghanistan appears undiminished, even if at least momentarily marked by self-interested restraint. More than anything, the failure of the current U.S. approach to Iran to achieve its aims reflects the complexity and intractability of this problem, which has frustrated U.S. officials from both sides of the political aisle for nearly thirty years.

The polarized American political climate has tended to discourage sober, evenhanded analysis of the Bush approach to Iran, as any balanced appraisals are drowned out by right-wing castigation of any steps short of Iran's isolation and left-wing fear-mongering about the administration's supposed inexorable press for war. Inevitably, the reality is far more nuanced. In considering the Bush diplomacy on Iran and its results, there is obviously much to critique.

Most of the administration's failings can be traced back to the spectacularly misinformed assumptions about Iran and the region that senior U.S. officials nurtured even in the face of contradictory evidence—the presumptions that the Islamic Republic was on the verge of collapse, that intensifying concerns about Iran would fundamentally alter the strategic calculus of the leading Arab states, and that a belated effort to engage Tehran could succeed while maintaining the posture and rhetoric of regime change. These misapprehensions are the product of an incredibly limited knowledge base within the U.S. government about Iran as well as the antipathy of the Bush administration to questioning its own ideological verities. Secretary Rice acknowledged this in June 2007, telling the *Wall Street Journal* editorial board that the Islamic Republic is "a political system I don't understand very well," adding that "one of the downsides of not having been in Iran . . . for twenty-seven years as a government is that we don't really have people who know Iran inside our own system. . . . We're also operating from something of a disadvantage in that we don't really have very good veracity or a feel for the place."[1] Seven years after September 11, and nearly three decades after the Iranian revolution, there is simply no justification for this kind of amateurishness in U.S. policy toward such a critical actor.

At the same time, the administration also deserves some credit in specific areas—for engaging in the thankless, dogged toil of building and sustaining a surprisingly robust international coalition on Iran; for endeavoring to reverse certain elements of its policy when it was clearly required; and for crafting a serious diplomatic overture to Iran on its nuclear program. To its credit, the administration also recognized that the U.S. diplomatic apparatus for dealing with Iran was insufficient and dysfunctional, the victim of the long American absence from Tehran and bureaucratic neglect, and in response, establishing a new set of administrative structures to coordinate all official policy and activities with respect to Iran. Over the long term, the new configuration is intended to create a cadre of U.S. officials skilled in interpreting Iranian issues and capable of staffing some future diplomatic engagement.

In addition, the administration notably placed a priority on reenergizing people-to-people diplomacy, a particularly constructive move. In the wake of the catastrophic December 2003 earthquake near the southeastern city of Bam, Washington quickly mobilized a massive relief package. Sanctions prohibiting transfers and technology to Iran were also eased to facilitate the work of nongovernmental organizations at the disaster site. The following year, the Librarian of Congress traveled to Iran and signed an agreement to exchange materials with Iran's national library. The much vaunted democracy program launched in 2004 incorporated only a relatively small sum ($5 million) for expanding exchanges, but high-level U.S. government interest and the realities of the current environment in Iran are likely to swing much of the democracy programming toward greater emphasis on people-to-people exchanges.

---

1.   Secretary of State Condoleezza Rice, interview by *Wall Street Journal* editorial board, June 8, 2007, www.state.gov/secretary/rm/2007/06/86254.htm (accessed April 17, 2008).

With these limited achievements, though, a new U.S. administration will face an enormous challenge in trying to devise an effective approach to Iran. Washington should begin with the caveat that panaceas have no place in managing U.S. policy toward Tehran. Both Americans and Iranians occasionally indulge in fantasies that some "grand bargain" can be achieved that will holistically settle all of the outstanding issues between the two governments. Unfortunately, however, history demonstrates that the depth of the grievances and the complexity of the political contexts on both sides obstructs even the slightest positive movement. Short of a wholesale political transformation in Tehran, there is no magic formula for settling this rift.

The United States needs to embrace this reality, just as key Iranian officials have come to do. "U.S.-Iranian relations are not something that can be fixed with one person saying one thing and everything will be okay," said Jalili, secretary of Iran's Supreme National Security Committee. "This relationship needs fundamental changes."[2] He has been echoed by former foreign minister Ali Akbar Velayati, an influential adviser to the supreme leader who has been part of Iran's decision-making structure since the earliest days of the revolution. "The domestic mind-set that negotiations with America will solve all our problems is a mirage," Velayati has asserted. "Those people who have gotten overexcited about the fact that negotiations with America will be the cure to all problems have miscalculated."[3]

The United States may not be in a position to draft a comprehensive settlement, or even—given the uncertainties of the upcoming months—a credible road map for revising U.S. policy toward Iran. However, the United States can identify a series of general principles that should frame strategy if it is to be successful. First, and most importantly, a successful American approach to Iran must acknowledge that diplomacy is the only alternative available to U.S. policymakers. The United States simply does not have a viable military option available that would generate a better outcome for U.S. interests across the Middle East. Any resort to force to address concerns about Iran's nuclear program or its involvement in terrorism would significantly harm primary objectives in the region. Iranian leaders learned from Iraq's Osirak experience, and as a result their nuclear installations are hardened, dispersed, and located near population centers. Moreover, given the failures of U.S. intelligence in Iraq, there is little reason for confidence that any American strike would conclusively incapacitate Iran's nuclear program.

---

2.   Said Jalili, interview by Morteza Qamari Vafa and Akram Sharifi, Fars News Agency, March 7, 2007, www.farsnews.com/newstext.php?nn=8512130522 (accessed May 9, 2008).

3.   Ali Akbar Velayati, interview broadcast on the Vision of the Islamic Republic of Iran Network 2 on May 17, 2007, World News Connection.

Whatever limited benefits could be achieved in terms of delaying Iran's capacity to cross the nuclear threshold would be overwhelmingly offset by a wide range of negative consequences. A strike would galvanize Iran's profoundly nationalistic population and thoroughly consolidate public support for their unpopular government. The regime's retaliatory reach would be felt throughout the region, particularly by U.S. allies, and the aftermath would almost surely doom any prospects for revitalizing the peace process or wresting a stable outcome from Iraq. The sole beneficiaries from a military conflict between Washington and Tehran would be the forces of radical anti-Americanism throughout the Islamic world.

It has become axiomatic among U.S. officials and politicians that the military option does and should remain on the table for dealing with Tehran. This conventional wisdom warrants questioning. In reality, barring dramatic new developments, the military option is already off the table, courtesy in part of the intense press and public scrutiny of Washington's Iran policy that came in the wake of U.S. stumbling in Iraq. Most notably, the November 2007 release of the U.S. intelligence community's assessment that Iran in 2003 halted the weaponization component of its nuclear program transformed the debate and the decision-making context along with it. The prevailing—and not wholly accurate—interpretation of the report asserted that Iran's nuclear program no longer remained a threat. By eliminating any prospect of broad-based public or international support, the assessment obviated the possibility of a preemptive strike by the Bush administration. Threatening military action under these circumstances makes a mockery of American credibility.

Nonetheless, whoever succeeds President Bush is very likely to revisit the dilemma of coercive discourse as a way of dissuading Iran from its current course and persuading U.S. allies to utilize their leverage with Tehran. Washington needs to consider carefully the impact of American rhetoric on Iran's internal political dynamics. It is not clear that the vague references to American willingness to use force carry significant credibility in Tehran given the logistical and policy constraints that stem from U.S. involvements elsewhere in the region. Moreover, embellished by references to "World War III" and "nuclear holocaust" by the U.S. president, such rhetoric serves only to strengthen Iranian hard-liners and reinforce the most paranoid fears of a leadership already steeped in suspicion of American motives and objectives.

For all those Iranian political actors, such as Ahmadinejad, who have dismissed the possibility of a U.S. military strike on the country, there are others from each end of the political spectrum who have expressed fears that a desperate Washington might attack Iran to vindicate and/or extricate itself from its failed intervention in Iraq. "The Americans have faced a strategic dead end in Iraq, and due to the humiliating defeat they have faced in pursuing their Greater Middle East Initiative, they might be after new adventurism in Lebanon or Iran, for which both the Iranian Revolutionary Guard Corps (IRGC) and the Lebanese Hezbollah are fortunately well prepared," warned former Revolutionary Guards commander Rahim Safavi.[4]

The second principle that should anchor any new approach to Iran is an abiding commitment to engagement as one of the indispensable instruments of U.S. statecraft. As Iran's politics have shifted in a more radical right-wing direction, the appeal of engagement might seem to have diminished even to those who advocated it during the brief advent of a reformist president and parliament during the late 1990s. However, the best argument for engaging with Iran was never predicated on the relative palatability of potential interlocutors, but on the seriousness of the differences between governments and the centrality of the U.S. interests at stake. The international reprobation aimed at Ahmadinejad and his clique is well earned, and yet it is ultimately an insufficient excuse for constraining the U.S. government's own tools for dealing with Tehran. It is both appropriate and potentially effective to engage with Iran even when it is led by individuals whose views and policies the United States reviles.

The aim of diplomacy is to advance interests not to make friends or endorse enemies. Since Iran's revolution, each U.S. administration, across both political parties, has endorsed the use of dialogue and direct contact with Iran as a means of addressing American interests and concerns. The single exception entails a three-year period following the May 2003 decision by the Bush administration to curtail direct, bilateral discussions with Tehran on Afghanistan. Yet even the Bush administration later reversed this stance and made a serious diplomatic approach to Iran in May 2006 with its offer to negotiate on the nuclear program. That overture misfired, in large part due to the mistrust and hostility engendered by the administration's prior rebuff and embrace of regime change. The failure of the United States' 2006 offer only reinforces the importance of maintaining the long-standing receptivity to serious, authoritative dialogue with the Iranian leadership.

Engagement with Iran is not an automatic path to rapprochement, nor should it imply a unilateral offer of a "grand bargain." Rather it would entail a return to the long-held position that Amerca is prepared to talk with Iranian leaders, in a serious and sustained way, in any authoritative dialogue as a means of addressing the profound concerns that its policies pose for U.S. interests and allies. A commitment to engagement with Iran should also incorporate the designation of an authorized and empowered negotiator and outline a diplomatic process for making progress on the discrete but complex array of issues at stake. One possible mechanism worth pursuing derives

---

4. "Strategy Revision Was a Necessity at IRGC—Commander," Islamic Republic News Agency, August 17, 2007.

from a 2004 Council on Foreign Relations task force chaired by former national security adviser Zbigniew Brzezinski and Defense Secretary Robert Gates, serving at the time as president of Texas A&M University. The task force recommended outlining a basic statement of principles, along the lines of the 1972 Shanghai Communiqué signed by the United States and China, to provide the parameters for U.S.-Iranian engagement and establish the overarching objectives for dialogue.

It is equally important to note that in the absence of any purposeful commitment to engaging with Iran, the Bush administration's overreliance on sticks has inevitably proven ineffective as a means of altering Iran's behavior. Incremental international pressure, particularly while the costs are generally bearable, is more likely to consolidate the regime than splinter it, and Iran is more likely to escalate than concede when backed into a corner. Ultimately, the failure of the administration's diplomatic initiative should not discredit diplomacy as a tool for dealing with Tehran. In fact, it is the administration's early experience with the Geneva track dialogue with Tehran that should prove instructive about the potential payoffs of a serious effort to engage Iran.

Engaging with Iran will not be easy, nor will it provide immediate payoffs. Even during the heyday of the reform movement, Washington found little success in persuading Iran to engage in a direct and ongoing dialogue. Tehran ignored the quiet overtures of the Clinton administration and its predecessors, rebuffed efforts to address constructively outstanding issues such as the 1996 Khobar Towers bombing, and publicly disparaged the very U.S. gestures—including the March 2000 relaxation of U.S. sanctions on caviar, carpets, and pistachios—that were intended to show goodwill.[5] For the many justified critics of the subsequent administration's approach to Iran, President Clinton's experience should serve as a reminder that the United States should avoid the suggestion that it is solely responsible for the perpetuation of the estrangement or that the intensification of the Iranian challenge rests solely on the misjudgments of this administration or the United States alone. Engagement can be a powerful tool for dealing with Iran, but U.S. officials cannot know if or when they will find an authoritative interlocutor on the Iranian side.

Engaging with the Iranian regime does not imply forsaking U.S. commitment to criticizing Tehran's abuses of its citizens' rights. The United States can and should speak out in favor of greater social, political, and economic liberalization in Iran, and should object vigorously to the regime's repression—greatly increased in recent months—of dissidents, activists, and students. In lieu of its high-profile, low-impact democracy program, the United

---

5.   See Pollack, *The Persian Puzzle*, 325, for an account of the Clinton administration's June 1999 effort to encourage Iran to bring those responsible for the Khobar Towers bombing to justice.

States should dramatically expand opportunities for Iranians to interact with the rest of the world through exchange programs, scholarships, and enhanced access to visas.

The third principle that the United States must adopt is to drive a stake through the heart of the myth of externally orchestrated regime change. This is no small task—there is much to suggest that the Islamic Republic is vulnerable, and the illusion of an imminent revolution has tempted U.S. administrations and pundits repeatedly over the past three decades. For the Bush administration, indulging in the misapprehension produced several years of diplomatic inaction and a stream of fruitless and counterproductive public messaging, and eventually tainted even its belated but genuine efforts to initiate dialogue with Tehran. Secretary Rice was forced to resort to a grudging public acknowledgment that the administration was not seeking regime change, but it was too little and too late to alter the strategic calculus of a regime whose leadership viewed the United States as irrevocably opposed to its existence.

Abandoning the regime change fantasy means disbanding or significantly retooling democracy promotion programming for Iran. After a thirty-year absence and with only the haziest sense of the day-to-day dynamics of the Islamic Republic's politics and society, Washington is unlikely to succeed in attempting to conjure up an opposition or orchestrate political mobilization from a distance. Failure, however, is hardly the worst-case outcome here; the publicity surrounding the U.S. democracy program has already helped spark a revived crackdown on Iranian dissidents and activists and has constrained and undermined the very civil society the United States hopes to support. Even among the most ardent opponents of the Islamic regime, accepting support from an external government remains highly taboo simply because it contravenes one of the authentic tenets of the revolution that remains largely unrepudiated—Iran's struggle for independence from the machinations of foreign powers. The country's most prominent dissidents have repeatedly condemned the U.S. funding, arguing as a famed journalist and former political prisoner did in the *Washington Post*, "The Bush administration may be striving to help Iranian democrats, but any Iranian who seeks American dollars will not be recognized as a democrat by his or her fellow citizens."[6] As a result of this renunciation as well as the formidable logistical obstacles to funneling support to Iranian oppositionists, it remains unclear how much—if any—of the millions already appropriated for the Iran democracy program will ever reach Iranians.

Official U.S. efforts to promote democracy around the world reflect a strategic imperative, particularly in the post-9/11 era, as well as a domestic political calculation. And it is understandable that the precedents of U.S. assistance

---

6.   Akbar Ganji, "Why Iran's Democrats Shun Aid," *Washington Post*, October 26, 2007.

to fledgling movements in Serbia, Ukraine, Georgia, and elsewhere prompt an interest in replicating success—even if there is a tendency to overstate the American role in these episodes and to disregard subsequent regressions in several cases. However, policy measures must be judged on their prospective utility, and the reaction of Iranian dissidents to U.S. funding reflect the unique context that inevitably frames this initiative. The notion of American meddling in Iran's internal affairs represents the third rail of Iranian politics, a legacy of the infamous U.S. role in the 1953 coup that unseated Prime Minister Muhammad Mussadiq. This episode fostered an obsessive resentment of Washington and crystallized a "conspiratorial interpretation of politics" that "permeates [Iranian] society, the mainstream as much as the fringe, and cuts through all sectors of the political spectrum."[7]

Finally, America must recognize that the ideal opportunity for dealing with Tehran will never come; the objective of U.S. policy must be to create the grounds for progress with Iran even if the Iranian internal environment remains hostile or the regional context continues to present challenges. The Bush administration first embraced a chimerical notion of the regime's vulnerability and later boxed itself into a corner by insisting that nothing could be achieved so long as the Iranians perceived momentum to be on their side. Secretary Rice brushed off congressional queries about dialogue with Iran over Iraq in January 2007, saying that approaching Tehran while neighboring Iraq was still in turmoil would be counterproductive. "[If we] go to the Iranians and as supplicants say to the Iranians, help us to secure Iraq, do we really believe that the Iranians are going to treat Iraq over here and not demand that we do something to alleviate the pressure that we're now bringing on their nuclear program and their nuclear ambitions? I don't think it's going to happen."[8]

Timing matters in negotiations, and the concern about the impact of regional dynamics is justifiable, but to avoid diplomatic interface because of a perceived power imbalance is effectively to consign the countries to permanent antagonism. The U.S. interest in addressing the challenges posed by Iran cannot be deferred until the United States has achieved the most conducive regional balance of power or until Iran has finally elected the most amenable array of leaders.

Each of these recommendations has an important associated benefit— each would complement the U.S. efforts to rebuild its relationships with the broader Muslim world. This is a multilevel process—we must address the Iranian threat convincingly and help mitigate concerns about a Shia "arc of

---

7.   Abrahamian, *Khomeinism: Essays*, 112.
8.   Secretary of State Condoleezza Rice, "Iraq: A New Way Forward," testimony before the House Foreign Affairs Committee, January 11, 2007, www.state.gov/secretary/rm/2007/78640.htm (accessed April 17, 2008).

conflict" in the region. But Americans must also recognize the reverbera-tions of U.S. actions and rhetoric around the region. This is particularly the case where U.S. government rhetoric is concerned; the citizens of the wider Islamic world are generally sophisticated enough to sense the hypocrisy in-herent in U.S. praise of small steps toward political competition in Egypt and castigation of Iran's flawed ballot as a "sham election."

American influence may be limited but the potential rewards are not. A democratic, peaceful Iran would have a profound influence over regional and doctrinal debates. The domino effect of democracy that optimistic prognosti-cators applied to U.S. intervention in Iraq might actually be valid in the case of Iran, if only because its political history and climate is more conducive to the competition of democratic elections.

For nearly three decades, U.S.-Iranian relations have been entangled in an emotional crisis defying the common interests that the two states share. For Iran, America remains a state that persistently interferes in its internal affairs, delegitimizes its electoral process, and actively calls for a change in its regime. For America, Iran is frozen in time, a state that egregiously vio-lated international law and held fifty-two Americans captive for 444 days, and continues to plot against U.S. interests throughout the Middle East. The unfortunate tendency to conflate Ahmadinejad with Hitler in both discourse and policy prescriptions promotes an image of Iran's leadership as genocidal, irrational, and undeterrable.[9] This sort of rhetoric may be satisfying in con-veying appropriate outrage at the Iranian president's rhetoric, but it is neither accurate nor conducive to a serious appraisal of U.S. policy options.

Such exaggerations and distortions have been the currency of U.S.-Iranian discourse, conditioning and reinforcing the two sides' antagonism. The best manner of moving forward is recognition that Iran is not an emotional crisis to come to terms with, but a strategic problem to be managed.

---

9.   "Ahmadinejad Is 'Persian Hitler': Israel's Peres," Agence France-Presse, November 16, 2006.

Index

About the Author

Suzanne Maloney is a senior fellow at the Brookings Institution's Saban Center for Middle East Policy and formerly served on the policy-planning staff of the State Department.

United States Institute of Peace

The United States Institute of Peace is an independent, nonpartisan institution established and funded by Congress. Its goals are to help prevent and resolve violent conflicts, promote post-conflict peacebuilding, and increase conflict-management tools, capacity, and intellectual capital worldwide. The Institute does this by empowering others with knowledge, skills, and resources, as well as by directly engaging in peacebuilding projects around the globe.

Chairman of the Board: J. Robinson West
Vice Chairman: María Otero
President: Richard H. Solomon
Executive Vice President: Patricia Powers Thomson
Vice President: Charles E. Nelson

Board of Directors

J. Robinson West (Chairman), Chairman, PFC Energy, Washington, D.C.

María Otero (Vice Chairman), President, ACCION International, Boston, Mass.

Holly J. Burkhalter, Vice President of Government Affairs, International Justice Mission, Washington, D.C.

Anne H. Cahn, Former Scholar in Residence, American University, Washington, D.C.

Chester A. Crocker, James R. Schlesinger Professor of Strategic Studies, School of Foreign Service, Georgetown University, Washington, D.C.

Laurie S. Fulton, Partner, Williams and Connolly, Washington, D.C.

Charles Horner, Senior Fellow, Hudson Institute, Washington, D.C.

Kathleen Martinez, Executive Director, World Institute on Disability, Oakland, Calif.

George E. Moose, Adjunct Professor of Practice, The George Washington University, Washington, D.C.

Jeremy A. Rabkin, Professor of Law, George Mason University, Fairfax, Va.

Ron Silver, Actor, Producer, Director, Primparous Productions, Inc.

Judy Van Rest, Executive Vice President, International Republican Institute, Washington, D.C.

Members ex officio

David Kramer, Assistant Secretary of the Bureau of Democracy, Human Rights, and Labor, Department of State

Christopher "Ryan" Henry, Principal Deputy Under Secretary for Policy, Department of Defense

Richard H. Solomon, President, United States Institute of Peace (nonvoting)

Frances C. Wilson, Lieutenant General, U.S. Marine Corps; President, National Defense University

Iran's Long Reach

Text: Palatino and Optima

Display Text: Cochin and ITC Symbol Std.

Cover Design: Hasten Design Studio and Cynthia Jordan

Interior Design and Page Makeup: Katharine Moore

Developmental Editor: Kurt Volkan

Copyediting: Paul Morro

Proofreading: Amy Thompson

Indexing: Potomac Indexing

Pivotal States in the Muslim World

As part of its Muslim World Initiative, the United States Institute of Peace's Center for Conflict Analysis and Prevention is undertaking a major analytical effort in which leading scholars and area specialists measure the influence of certain pivotal states on the broader Muslim world and assess how their political and social evolution will affect U.S. interests across the Muslim world.

This collective initiative builds on the argument put forth by Robert Chase, Emily Hill, and Paul Kennedy in 1996 that the United States should prioritize the application of its limited resources and attention toward so-called pivotal states. As they argue, such states merit particular attention because they affect—both positively and negatively—not only the stability of their respective regions but also of the larger international system. Here, focusing specifically on pivotal Muslim states and U.S. interests in the Muslim world, this project aims to identify which states in the Muslim world are most influential and critical to U.S. foreign policy. The Muslim world, for purposes of this project, includes not only states with Muslim majorities (such as Pakistan, Indonesia, Iran, and Saudi Arabia) but also states with important Muslim minorities (such as India, France, Germany, and Russia).

This volume, Graham Fuller's *The New Turkish Republic: Turkey as a Pivotal State in Muslim World*, and John N. Paden's *Faith and Politics in Nigeria: Nigeria as a Pivotal State in the Muslim World* are products of this initiative.